EASY MEALS IN MINUTES

150 Tasty Recipes in 30 Minutes or Less

TIME-LIFE BOOKS, ALEXANDRIA, VIRGINIA

TIME-LIFE BOOKS IS A DIVISION OF TIME LIFE INC.

Easy Meals in Minutes
Project Manager   Donia Steele
Vice President of Sales and Marketing   Neil Levin
Director of Special Sales   Liz Ziehl
Production Manager   Carolyn Mills Bounds
Quality Assurance Manager   James King

Produced by Rebus, Inc.
New York, New York

Photographers: Alan Richardson, Christopher Lawrence, Ellen Silverman, Elizabeth Watt, Steven Mays, Steven Mark Needham

Easy Meals in Minutes is an adaptation of Creative Everyday Cooking.

First printing.
Printed in U.S.A.

TIME-LIFE is a trademark of Time Warner Inc. U.S.A.

Library of Congress Cataloging–in–Publication Data

Easy meals in minutes: 150 tasty recipes in 30 minutes or less.
    p.   cm.
Includes index.
ISBN 0-7835-5287-4
    1. Entrées (Cookery).   2. Quick and easy cookery.   I. Time-Life Books.
TX740.E28   1998
641.8'2--dc21   97-22428
                                                                        CIP

Books produced by Time-Life Custom Publishing are available at special bulk discount for promotional and premium use. Custom adaptations can also be created to meet your specific marketing goals. Call 1-800-323-5255.

CONTENTS

Pasta with No-Cook Herb Tomato Sauce (page 25)

CHAPTER 1
PASTA

Pasta Shells with Salmon and Lemon-Dill Sauce

▼

The quick trick here: Rather than thawing the frozen peas called for in the recipe, simply place them in a colander and drain the pasta over them. The boiling-hot pasta water thaws and heats the peas to perfection. And the lemon-dill sauce is nearly as quick to make, whirled for a few seconds in a food processor. Toss the pasta, sauce and salmon lightly, so the fish remains in generous chunks.

Working time: 5 minutes
Total time: 25 minutes

Pasta Shells with Salmon and Lemon-Dill Sauce

6 Servings

2 packages (3 ounces each) cream cheese

1 cup plain yogurt

1 tablespoon lemon juice

1 tablespoon grated lemon zest (optional)

¼ teaspoon pepper

⅓ cup chopped fresh dill or 2 teaspoons dried

2 cups small pasta shells (about ½ pound)

1 package (10 ounces) frozen peas

2 cans (7½ ounces each) salmon, drained

Step 2

1 Bring a large pot of water to a boil.

2 Meanwhile, in a food processor blend the cream cheese, yogurt, lemon juice, lemon zest (if using) and pepper until smooth. Stir in the dill.

3 Add the pasta to the boiling water and cook until al dente, 10 to 12 minutes, or according to package directions.

4 Place the frozen peas in a colander and when the pasta is done, pour the pasta and boiling water over the peas.

5 Transfer the pasta and peas to a serving bowl. Add the salmon and lemon-dill sauce and toss gently.

Step 4

TIME-SAVERS

■ *Microwave tip: To bring cold cream cheese quickly to room temperature (which makes it easier to blend), place the unwrapped cream cheese on a microwave-safe plate. Microwave at 50% for 1 minute or until softened.*

■ *Do-ahead: The lemon-dill sauce (Step 2) can be made ahead.*

Values are approximate per serving: Calories: 384   Protein: 24 gm   Fat: 14 gm
Carbohydrates: 39 gm   Cholesterol: 56 mg   Sodium: 454 mg

Step 5

Penne with Peppers, White Beans and Thyme

Pasta and beans are a favorite Italian pairing, as in the well-known "pasta e fagioli." And this tasty dish offers a nutritional bonus: a generous amount of no-cholesterol protein, thanks to the combination of grain products with legumes. If you're trying to cut down on fat and calories, omit the butter, or just use one tablespoon instead of two. If you can't find a yellow bell pepper, use a second green pepper or a red pepper.

Working time: 20 minutes
Total time: 25 minutes

Penne with Peppers, White Beans and Thyme

6 Servings

1 medium red onion
1 large green bell pepper
1 large yellow bell pepper
3 tablespoons olive or other vegetable oil
3 cloves garlic, minced or crushed through a press
½ pound penne or other medium-large tube pasta (about 2¼ cups)

1 can (16 ounces) small white beans
2 tablespoons lemon juice
1 teaspoon thyme
¾ teaspoon salt
¼ teaspoon black pepper
2 tablespoons butter

Step 5

1 Bring a large pot of water to a boil.

2 Meanwhile, cut the onion into thin slices. Cut the bell peppers into bite-size pieces.

3 In a large skillet, warm 2 tablespoons of the oil over medium-high heat until hot but not smoking. Add the onion and garlic, and sauté until the onion begins to brown, about 5 minutes.

4 Add the pasta to the boiling water and cook until al dente, 10 to 12 minutes, or according to package directions.

5 Meanwhile, add the remaining 1 tablespoon oil to the skillet. Add the bell peppers and cook, stirring, for 5 minutes.

Step 6

6 Rinse the beans under running water and drain well. Add the beans, lemon juice, thyme, salt and black pepper to the skillet and cook over medium-high heat until the beans are heated through, about 3 minutes. Remove from the heat.

7 Drain the pasta and toss it with the butter. Toss the pasta and the vegetable mixture together to combine.

TIME-SAVERS

■ *Do-ahead:* The bean mixture can be made a short time ahead and left at room temperature. Reheat the beans gently or let the freshly cooked hot pasta warm them up.

Step 7

Values are approximate per serving: Calories: 339 Protein: 11 gm Fat: 12 gm
Carbohydrates: 49 gm Cholesterol: 10 mg Sodium: 323 mg

Meat Ravioli in Hearty Mushroom Broth

▼

*You don't need a heavy sauce to turn meat ravioli into a hearty meal:
Here, a deep-flavored mushroom broth sets off the filled pasta to perfection.
If you can't find meat ravioli—or simply prefer a variation—you
could also prepare this dish with cheese ravioli, but substitute white wine for
the red and chicken broth for the beef broth.*

Working time: 15 minutes
Total time: 25 minutes

Meat Ravioli in Hearty Mushroom Broth

6 Servings

1 medium onion
½ pound mushrooms
2 tablespoons olive or other vegetable oil
2 cloves garlic, minced or crushed through a press
2 tablespoons flour
1¾ cups beef broth

⅓ cup dry red wine
3 tablespoons chopped parsley (optional)
1 teaspoon basil
¼ teaspoon pepper
1 pound meat ravioli (about 3 dozen)

Step 2

1 Thinly slice the onion. Quarter the mushrooms.

2 In a large saucepan, warm the oil over medium-high heat until hot but not smoking. Add the garlic and onion and cook, stirring, until the onion begins to brown, about 3 minutes.

3 Add the mushrooms and cook, stirring, until the mushrooms are lightly coated with oil, about 1 minute.

4 Stir in the flour and cook, stirring, until the flour is no longer visible, about 30 seconds. Add the beef broth, wine, parsley (if using), basil and pepper, and bring to a boil over medium-high heat.

Step 4

5 Add the ravioli and cook until al dente, 8 to 10 minutes, or according to package directions.

6 Spoon the broth into individual bowls and serve the ravioli on top.

Values are approximate per serving: Calories: 307 Protein: 13 gm Fat: 15 gm
Carbohydrates: 28 gm Cholesterol: 59 mg Sodium: 564 mg

Step 5

Noodles and Mushrooms with Creamy Poppyseed Sauce

▼

*In Germany and Eastern Europe, noodles are more likely to be served with a
sour cream sauce, like this one, than with tomato sauce. Here, the noodles
are tossed with sautéed onions, mushrooms and a sour cream-yogurt sauce flavored
with lemon zest and poppyseeds. If you have time, toast the poppyseeds in an
ungreased skillet for a few seconds to bring out their nutlike taste.*

Working time: 20 minutes
Total time: 30 minutes

4 Servings

2 medium onions
½ pound mushrooms
2 tablespoons olive or other
   vegetable oil
2 cloves garlic, minced or crushed
   through a press
2 tablespoons butter
⅓ cup lemon juice
¾ teaspoon salt

½ teaspoon black pepper
Pinch of cayenne pepper
¾ pound medium egg noodles
⅓ cup sour cream
⅓ cup plain yogurt
2 tablespoons poppyseeds
1 tablespoon grated lemon zest
   (optional)

Step 1

1 Thinly slice the onions and the mushrooms.

2 In a medium skillet, warm the oil over medium-high heat until hot but not smoking. Add the onions and garlic, and cook until the onions begin to brown, about 5 minutes.

3 Bring a large pot of water to a boil.

4 Meanwhile, add the butter to the skillet and heat until melted. Add the mushrooms and cook until they begin to soften, about 5 minutes.

5 Add the lemon juice, salt, black and cayenne peppers to the skillet. Bring the mixture to a boil. Reduce the heat to low, cover and simmer while you cook the noodles.

Step 4

6 Add the noodles to the boiling water and cook until al dente, 4 to 6 minutes, or according to package directions.

7 Meanwhile, in a small bowl, combine the sour cream, yogurt, poppyseeds and lemon zest (if using).

8 Drain the noodles and place them in a serving bowl. Add the mushroom mixture and the sour cream mixture and toss to combine.

TIME-SAVERS

■ *Do-ahead: The mushroom mixture (Steps 1 through 5) and the sour cream mixture (Step 7) can be made ahead. If you refrigerate the mixtures, let them return to room temperature before combining with freshly cooked hot noodles.*

Step 8

Values are approximate per serving: Calories: 546 Protein: 16 gm Fat: 23 gm
Carbohydrates: 71 gm Cholesterol: 106 mg Sodium: 520 mg

Tortellini Salad with Lemon-Mustard Vinaigrette

▼

This colorful salad can be tossed together ahead of time and served at room temperature, making it an excellent choice for a holiday buffet or backyard picnic. You'll find boxes or bags of dried tortellini in some supermarkets; if you don't, try a gourmet shop or Italian grocery. The advantage of dried tortellini over fresh is that they keep at room temperature, ready for use on short notice.

Working time: 15 minutes
Total time: 25 minutes

Tortellini Salad with Lemon-Mustard Vinaigrette

4 Servings

2 tablespoons lemon juice
1 teaspoon grated lemon zest (optional)
¼ cup olive or other vegetable oil
1 tablespoon Dijon mustard
½ teaspoon dill
⅛ teaspoon salt
⅛ teaspoon black pepper
Pinch of sugar

1½ cups dried cheese-filled tortellini (about 6 ounces)
5 cherry tomatoes
1 small yellow or red bell pepper
1 small green bell pepper
1 small zucchini
Half a small red onion
3 scallions

Step 2

1 Bring a large pot of water to a boil.

2 Meanwhile, place the lemon juice and zest (if using) in a large salad bowl. Whisk in the oil, mustard, dill, salt, black pepper and sugar.

3 Add the pasta to the boiling water and cook until al dente, 10 to 12 minutes, or according to package directions.

4 Meanwhile, halve the cherry tomatoes. Cut the bell peppers into bite-size pieces. Cut the zucchini into matchsticks. Cut the onion into thin rings. Finely chop the scallions.

Step 4

5 Drain the pasta and add it to the vinaigrette in the serving bowl. Add the vegetables and toss well to combine. Serve the salad warm or at room temperature.

TIME-SAVERS

■ *Do-ahead: The vinaigrette can be made and the vegetables cut up ahead. Or, the entire salad can be made well ahead and served at room temperature or chilled. If you are making the salad ahead, toss it with only half of the vinaigrette, then toss it with the remaining dressing just before serving.*

Values are approximate per serving: Calories: 314   Protein: 10 gm   Fat: 17 gm
Carbohydrates: 32 gm   Cholesterol: 31 mg   Sodium: 440 mg

Step 5

Linguine with Spicy Parsley-Clam Sauce

▼

Hot red pepper flakes give this colorful clam sauce a new twist. If your family is not fond of spicy foods, add just ½ teaspoon of the pepper flakes to begin, then taste the sauce and add more pepper if you wish. For stronger clam flavor, use bottled clam juice in place of the chicken broth called for; but, since clam juice is saltier than chicken broth, you may want to omit the recipe's salt.

Working time: 15 minutes
Total time: 15 minutes

Linguine with Spicy Parsley-Clam Sauce

4 Servings

1 medium red onion
⅓ cup chopped parsley
2 tablespoons butter
2 tablespoons olive oil
4 cloves garlic, minced or crushed through a press
2 tablespoons flour
1 cup chicken broth

½ to 1 teaspoon red pepper flakes, to taste
¼ teaspoon black pepper
¼ teaspoon salt
½ pound linguine
2 cans (6 ounces each) chopped clams, drained
⅓ cup grated Parmesan cheese

1 Bring a large pot of water to a boil.

2 Meanwhile, thinly slice the onion and chop the parsley.

3 In a large skillet, melt the butter in the oil over medium heat. Add the garlic and onion and sauté until the onion is translucent and beginning to brown slightly, about 5 minutes.

Step 4

4 Add the flour and cook, stirring, until the flour is no longer visible, about 1 minute. Add the broth, red pepper flakes, black pepper and salt. Reduce the heat to medium-low, cover and simmer for 5 minutes.

5 Meanwhile, add the linguine to the boiling water and cook until al dente, 8 to 10 minutes or according to package directions.

6 When the pasta is ready, drain it in a colander. Add the chopped clams and parsley to the skillet. Then add the drained pasta and toss to combine.

Step 6

7 Serve the pasta with grated Parmesan on the side.

TIME-SAVERS

■ *Do-ahead: The sauce can be made ahead through Step 4 and reheated before tossing with the chopped clams and freshly cooked pasta.*

Step 6

Values are approximate per serving: Calories: 416 Protein: 20 gm Fat: 14 gm
Carbohydrates: 51 gm Cholesterol: 45 mg Sodium: 379 mg

Pasta Twists with Spicy Broccoli Sauce

▼

Stir-fried red bell pepper and broccoli give this pasta dinner a colorful look; garlic, red onion and hot pepper provide an inviting bite. For speed, the garlic, onion and bell pepper can be chopped in the food processor. The broccoli stems can also be chopped in the processor, but the tops should be cut up by hand. Although the heavy cream adds richness here, you can save on calories by using chicken broth in its place.

Working time: 25 minutes
Total time: 30 minutes

6 Servings

3 cloves garlic
1 medium red onion
2 medium stalks broccoli
1 large red bell pepper
¾ pound pasta twists (about 4½ cups)
2 tablespoons olive or other vegetable oil

¾ teaspoon oregano
½ teaspoon salt
¼ teaspoon red pepper flakes
¼ teaspoon black pepper
1 cup heavy cream
½ cup grated Parmesan cheese

1 Bring a large pot of water to a boil.

2 Meanwhile, in a food processor, finely chop the garlic. Add the onion and coarsely chop. Remove to a plate and set aside.

3 Separate the broccoli tops from the stems. Cut the stems and tops into bite-size pieces. In the food processor, coarsely chop the bell pepper.

Step 3

4 Add the pasta to the boiling water and cook until al dente, 10 to 12 minutes, or according to package directions.

5 Meanwhile, in a large skillet, warm 1 tablespoon of the oil over medium-high heat until hot but not smoking. Add the garlic-onion mixture and stir-fry until browned, about 5 minutes.

6 Add the remaining 1 tablespoon oil, the broccoli tops and stems, the bell pepper, oregano, salt, red pepper flakes and black pepper. Stir-fry until the vegetables are crisp-tender, about 5 minutes.

7 Add the heavy cream and Parmesan and bring the mixture to a gentle boil over medium heat. Cook, stirring, until the mixture thickens slightly, 2 to 3 minutes.

Step 6

8 Drain the pasta and toss with the vegetables and sauce.

TIME-SAVERS

■ *Do-ahead: The vegetables can be cut up and the sauce made through Step 6 ahead of time.*

Values are approximate per serving: Calories: 493 Protein: 18 gm Fat: 23 gm
Carbohydrates: 58 gm Cholesterol: 60 mg Sodium: 388 mg

Step 7

Spinach Pasta with Cauliflower-Cheddar Sauce

▼

When making a pasta-and-vegetable dish, cook the vegetables in the same pot with the pasta; you'll save both time and energy. The flavorful sauce for this dish is made with sharp Cheddar cheese. Look for a well-aged Cheddar; using your palate and pocketbook as your guides, choose one from New York State, Wisconsin or Vermont, or select an imported English cheese.

Working time: 10 minutes
Total time: 20 minutes

Spinach Pasta with Cauliflower-Cheddar Sauce

8 Servings

1 small head cauliflower (about
  1¾ pounds)
¾ pound spinach fettuccine
4 tablespoons butter
2 cloves garlic, minced or crushed
  through a press
⅓ cup flour

½ cup chicken broth
1 cup milk
2 cups grated sharp Cheddar
  cheese (about ½ pound)
3 tablespoons Dijon mustard
¼ teaspoon pepper

Step 3

1 Bring a large pot of water to a boil.

2 Meanwhile, cut the cauliflower into bite-size pieces.

3 Add the pasta to the boiling water and cook until al dente, 10 to 12 minutes, or according to package directions. Add the cauliflower to the pasta water 5 minutes before the pasta is done.

4 Meanwhile, in a medium saucepan, melt the butter over medium heat. Add the garlic and cook for 1 minute.

5 Stirring constantly, add the flour and cook until the flour absorbs all the butter. Then slowly pour in the chicken broth and stir until smooth.

Step 5

6 Blend in the milk, Cheddar, mustard and pepper, and stir until the cheese is melted.

7 Drain the pasta and cauliflower and toss them with the cheese sauce.

TIME-SAVERS

■ *Microwave tip: For the sauce, place the butter and garlic in a 4-cup glass measure. Cook at 100% for 1 minute, or until the butter melts. Stir in the flour, then gradually add the broth. Stir in the milk, mustard and pepper. Cook at 100% for 3 minutes, or until hot. Stir in the Cheddar and cook at 50% for 3 minutes, or until the cheese is melted, stirring once.*

Step 6

Values are approximate per serving: Calories: 384 Protein: 16 gm Fat: 19 gm
Carbohydrates: 39 gm Cholesterol: 90 mg Sodium: 516 mg

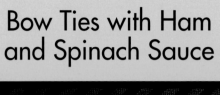

Bow Ties with Ham and Spinach Sauce

▼

*An interesting interplay of flavors and textures enlivens this pasta dinner:
The spinach in the sauce is enhanced by a bit of nutmeg, and the creamy wine sauce
itself provides a perfect backdrop for strips of smoked ham. It takes a few minutes
to reduce the sauce, but this is done while the pasta cooks, so no time is wasted. For a
variation, try fusilli or a tube-shaped pasta, such as penne, instead of bow ties.*

Working time: 20 minutes
Total time: 25 minutes

Bow Ties with Ham and Spinach Sauce

4 Servings

2 cloves garlic
4 shallots or 1 small onion
1 tablespoon butter
1 tablespoon olive or other vegetable oil
½ pound bow tie pasta (about 4 cups)
1 cup heavy cream

½ cup dry white wine or chicken broth
½ cup chicken broth
½ teaspoon nutmeg
¼ teaspoon pepper
1 package (10 ounces) frozen chopped spinach, thawed
½ pound smoked ham

1 Bring a large pot of water to a boil.

2 Meanwhile, in a food processor, mince the garlic. Add the shallots (or onion) and coarsely chop.

3 In a large skillet, warm the butter in the oil over medium heat until the butter is melted. Add the garlic-shallot mixture and cook, stirring, until the shallots begin to brown, about 5 minutes.

4 Add the pasta to the boiling water and cook until al dente, 10 to 12 minutes, or according to package directions.

5 Meanwhile, add the cream, white wine, chicken broth, nutmeg and pepper to the skillet. Bring the mixture to a boil, reduce the heat to low and cook for 5 minutes, stirring occasionally.

6 Squeeze the spinach dry in several layers of paper towel. Increase the heat under the sauce to medium-high and bring to a boil. Stir in the spinach and let the mixture return to a boil. Reduce the heat to low, cover and simmer, stirring occasionally, for 3 minutes, or until the spinach is cooked through.

7 Cut the ham into matchsticks.

8 Drain the pasta and toss with the ham and spinach sauce.

TIME-SAVERS

■ ***Microwave tip:*** *To thaw the spinach, remove any foil wrapping, place the spinach on a microwave-safe plate and cook at 100% for 4 minutes.*

Values are approximate per serving: Calories: 580 Protein: 22 gm Fat: 32 gm
Carbohydrates: 50 gm Cholesterol: 116 mg Sodium: 1046 mg

Step 5

Step 6

Step 7

Pasta with No-Cook Herb Tomato Sauce

▼

Any type of long, thin pasta strands would work nicely in this quick and easy hot-weather dish. There's spaghetti, of course, but you could also try vermicelli ("little worms," a thin spaghetti), angel hair (extra-thin spaghetti), or tagliarini (thin, square-cut noodles, usually sold fresh). The cooking times vary: Fresh pasta can take as little as two minutes, while spaghetti may require nine minutes or longer.

Working time: 15 minutes
Total time: 20 minutes

4 Servings

3 cloves garlic, peeled
½ cup (packed) fresh basil leaves or 2½ teaspoons dried
1 can (15 ounces) whole tomatoes, drained
6 fresh plum tomatoes or 9 whole canned tomatoes, well drained
¼ cup black olives (optional)
2 tablespoons olive or other vegetable oil

1 tablespoon lemon juice
2 teaspoons grated lemon zest (optional)
½ teaspoon salt
¼ teaspoon pepper
¾ pound tagliarini or linguine
½ pound smoked turkey, unsliced

Step 2

1 Bring a large pot of water to a boil. Add the garlic to the water (it will cook along with the pasta).

2 Meanwhile, in a food processor, coarsely chop the basil. Add the canned tomatoes and coarsely chop. Add the fresh tomatoes (or additional canned tomatoes, if using) and olives (if using), and finely chop.

3 Transfer the tomato mixture to a large serving bowl. Add the oil, lemon juice, lemon zest (if using), salt and pepper.

4 Add the pasta to the boiling water and cook until al dente—2 to 3 minutes for tagliarini, 7 to 9 minutes for linguine—or according to package directions.

5 Meanwhile, cut the turkey into small cubes and set aside.

Step 5

6 Drain the pasta well. Press the garlic through a garlic press (or mash it with a fork) and add it to the tomato mixture in the serving bowl. Add the pasta and turkey to the serving bowl and toss to combine the ingredients.

TIME-SAVERS

■ **Do-ahead:** *The turkey can be cubed and the sauce can be made ahead through Step 3.*

Step 6

Values are approximate per serving: Calories: 479 Protein: 24 gm Fat: 10 gm
Carbohydrates: 73 gm Cholesterol: 30 mg Sodium: 1033 mg

Fettuccine with Walnut Alfredo Sauce

▼

When creamy Alfredo sauce meets Genovese pesto, the result is an extraordinary topping for pasta. This new version of an Alfredo sauce—made with yogurt and light cream in place of the traditional heavy cream—is enriched with walnuts, basil, garlic and Parmesan for an irresistible flavor and a luxurious texture. You can serve this proudly to family or guests; it needs just a tossed salad to make it a meal.

Working time: 15 minutes
Total time: 20 minutes

4 Servings

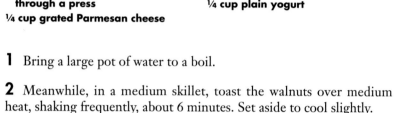

½ cup walnut pieces	¼ teaspoon salt
½ pound fettuccine	⅛ teaspoon pepper
¼ cup fresh basil leaves or 1 tablespoon dried basil	2 tablespoons olive or other vegetable oil
1 clove garlic, minced or crushed through a press	¼ cup light cream or half-and-half
¼ cup grated Parmesan cheese	¼ cup plain yogurt

1 Bring a large pot of water to a boil.

2 Meanwhile, in a medium skillet, toast the walnuts over medium heat, shaking frequently, about 6 minutes. Set aside to cool slightly.

Step 2

3 Add the pasta to the boiling water and cook until al dente, 8 to 10 minutes, or according to package directions.

4 Meanwhile, in a food processor, mince the basil and garlic. Add the walnuts, Parmesan, salt and pepper and process until just chopped.

5 With the processor running, add the oil. Then add the cream and yogurt.

6 Drain the pasta and toss it with the sauce.

TIME-SAVERS

■ *Microwave tip:* *To toast the walnuts, place them in a shallow microwave-safe bowl and drizzle with 1 teaspoon oil. Cook at 100% for 4 minutes, stirring once.*

Step 5

■ *Do-ahead:* *The walnuts can be toasted ahead. The sauce can be made ahead through Step 4.*

Values are approximate per serving: Calories: 437 Protein: 14 gm Fat: 23 gm
Carbohydrates: 46 gm Cholesterol: 69 mg Sodium: 258 mg

Step 6

Linguine and Broccoli with Peanut Sauce

▼

A favorite appetizer in Chinese restaurants is noodles with sesame sauce. You can create a similar, equally delicious entrée at home using peanut butter and Oriental sesame oil, which is available in many supermarkets. Broccoli, bell pepper and scallions round out this unusual pasta dish, complementing the velvety texture and rich flavors of the noodles and sauce.

Working time: 20 minutes
Total time: 25 minutes

Linguine and Broccoli with Peanut Sauce

6 Servings

½ cup plus 2 tablespoons creamy peanut butter
¼ cup reduced-sodium or regular soy sauce
2 tablespoons Oriental sesame oil
2 teaspoons distilled white vinegar
½ cup chicken broth
2 stalks broccoli

1 large red bell pepper
1 bunch scallions (6 to 8)
½ cup packed cilantro sprigs (optional)
½ pound linguine or spaghetti
2 tablespoons vegetable oil
3 cloves garlic, minced or crushed through a press

Step 2

1 Bring a large pot of water to a boil.

2 Meanwhile, in a food processor or blender, combine the peanut butter, soy sauce, sesame oil and vinegar, and blend until smooth. Gradually beat in the chicken broth until smooth.

3 Cut the broccoli and bell pepper into bite-size pieces. Coarsely chop the scallions and cilantro (if using).

4 Add the pasta to the boiling water and cook until al dente, 7 to 9 minutes, or according to package directions.

5 In a large skillet, warm the vegetable oil over medium-high heat until hot but not smoking. Add the garlic and cook for 1 minute, stirring frequently. Add the broccoli and bell pepper and stir-fry until the vegetables are just tender, 5 to 8 minutes.

Step 3

6 Stir the scallions and cilantro (if using) into the vegetables and remove the skillet from the heat.

7 Drain the pasta and toss it with the vegetables and peanut sauce.

TIME-SAVERS

■ *Do-ahead: The peanut sauce (Step 2) can be made ahead. The vegetables can be cut up ahead. The entire dish can also be made ahead and served at room temperature.*

Values are approximate per serving: Calories: 410 Protein: 15 gm Fat: 24 gm
Carbohydrates: 38 gm Cholesterol: 0 mg Sodium: 623 mg

Step 7

Linguine with Smoked Ham and Herb Butter

Heating herbs in butter brings out their full flavor; the butter then carries the herb flavor throughout the dish. Here, for a linguine sauce, butter is infused with fragrant basil, parsley and oregano (along with garlic and onions). Smoked ham, peas, yellow squash and carrots add substance and color to the dish. If smoked ham is not available, you can use regular boiled or baked ham—or smoked turkey or chicken.

Working time: 20 minutes
Total time: 25 minutes

Linguine with Smoked Ham and Herb Butter

6 Servings

3 cloves garlic
2 medium onions
¼ cup (packed) fresh basil leaves or
  2 teaspoons dried
¼ cup chopped parsley (optional)
3 medium carrots
1 medium yellow squash
½ pound smoked ham, unsliced

¾ pound linguine or spaghetti
4 tablespoons butter
1 tablespoon olive or other
  vegetable oil
2 teaspoons oregano
1 cup frozen peas, thawed
¼ teaspoon pepper

Step 3

1 Bring a large pot of water to a boil.

2 Meanwhile, in a food processor, mince the garlic. Add the onions and coarsely chop; set aside. In the same work bowl, mince the fresh basil and parsley (if using); set aside.

3 Cut the carrots and squash into thin slices. Cut the ham into ½-inch cubes.

4 Add the pasta to the boiling water and cook until al dente, 10 to 12 minutes, or according to package directions.

5 Meanwhile, in a large skillet, warm 2 tablespoons of the butter over medium-high heat until it is melted. Add the garlic-onion mixture and stir-fry until the onion begins to brown, about 3 minutes.

Step 6

6 Add the remaining 2 tablespoons butter, the olive oil, carrots, squash, basil, parsley and oregano. Cook, stirring, until the vegetables are almost tender, about 4 minutes.

7 Add the ham and peas, and cook, stirring, until the ham and peas are heated through and the vegetables are tender. Stir in the pepper.

8 Drain the pasta and toss with the ham and vegetable mixture.

TIME-SAVERS

■ **Do-ahead:** *The vegetables and ham can be cut up ahead.*

Step 7

Values are approximate per serving: Calories: 401   Protein: 17 gm   Fat: 13 gm
Carbohydrates: 54 gm   Cholesterol: 38 mg   Sodium: 664 mg

Fettuccine with Green Vegetables

▼

Although pasta cooks no more quickly in a microwave oven than it does on the stove, this time-saving appliance can often be used to streamline pasta sauces. The sauce here is made with frozen vegetables—spinach, peas and broccoli—which can be thawed in seconds in the microwave. They are then briefly sautéed and combined with sour cream, Parmesan and the pasta, putting dinner on the table in less than 30 minutes.

Working time: 15 minutes
Total time: 25 minutes

6 Servings

1 package (10 ounces) frozen chopped spinach
1 cup frozen peas
1 cup frozen chopped broccoli
½ pound fettuccine or other broad noodles
1 bunch scallions (6 to 8)
3 tablespoons butter

3 tablespoons olive or other vegetable oil
5 cloves garlic, minced or crushed through a press
¾ teaspoon salt
½ teaspoon pepper
1¼ cups sour cream
⅔ cup grated Parmesan cheese

1 Bring a large pot of water to a boil.

Step 2

2 Meanwhile, thaw the spinach, peas and broccoli in the microwave (one at a time). Set the broccoli and spinach aside on papers towels to drain as much excess moisture as possible. If the spinach is still watery, squeeze it between several layers of paper towels.

3 Add the pasta to the boiling water and cook until al dente, 10 to 12 minutes, or according to package directions.

4 Meanwhile, coarsely chop the scallions. In a large skillet, warm the butter in the oil over medium heat until the butter is melted. Add the scallions and garlic and sauté until the scallions are limp, about 5 minutes.

Step 5

5 Increase the heat to medium-high and add the spinach, peas, broccoli, salt and pepper. Cook, stirring, until the vegetables are heated through, about 5 minutes.

6 Stir in the sour cream and remove from the heat.

7 Drain the pasta and toss it with the vegetables and Parmesan.

TIME-SAVERS

■ *Do-ahead: The vegetables can be thawed and the sauce prepared through Step 4 ahead of time. Just before serving, cook the pasta and complete Steps 5 and 6 of the sauce.*

Step 6

Values are approximate per serving: Calories: 440 Protein: 14 gm Fat: 27 gm
Carbohydrates: 37 gm Cholesterol: 80 mg Sodium: 599 mg

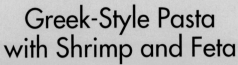
Greek-Style Pasta with Shrimp and Feta

▼

Feta cheese, a chalk-white cheese that originated in Greece, lends a Mediterranean air to this simple pasta and shrimp dish. Typically made from sheep's milk and preserved in brine, feta is quite salty. Prepackaged feta comes in small tubs of brine; if you buy a piece cut from a block, store it refrigerated and immersed in salted water. This type of cheese tastes best if used within a few days.

Working time: 30 minutes
Total time: 30 minutes

6 Servings

1 medium onion	**½ teaspoon basil**
2 tablespoons olive or other vegetable oil	**¼ teaspoon pepper**
3 cloves garlic, minced or crushed through a press	**¾ pound fettuccine**
2 cups canned whole tomatoes in tomato purée	**¾ pound medium shrimp**
1 teaspoon oregano	**½ cup pitted black olives**
	¼ pound feta cheese (about 1 cup crumbled), well drained

1 Bring a large pot of water to a boil.

2 Meanwhile, cut the onion into thin slices.

3 In a large skillet, warm the oil over medium-high heat until hot but not smoking. Add the onion and garlic and cook until the mixture is golden, about 5 minutes.

4 Add the tomatoes, oregano, basil and pepper, and bring the mixture to a boil over medium-high heat, breaking up the tomatoes with a spoon. Reduce the heat to low, cover and simmer, stirring occasionally, while you cook the pasta and prepare the shrimp.

5 Add the pasta to the boiling water and cook until al dente, 10 to 12 minutes, or according to package directions.

6 Meanwhile, shell and devein the shrimp.

7 Uncover the sauce and bring it to a boil over medium-high heat. Add the shrimp, reduce the heat to low, cover and simmer for 3 minutes.

8 Add the olives and half the feta cheese and stir to combine.

9 Drain the pasta and serve topped with the shrimp and sauce. Crumble the remaining feta cheese on top.

TIME-SAVERS

■ *Do-ahead: The sauce can be made ahead through Step 4. The shrimp can be shelled and deveined ahead.*

Values are approximate per serving: Calories: 396 Protein: 21 gm Fat: 13 gm Carbohydrates: 49 gm Cholesterol: 141 mg Sodium: 510 mg

Step 4

Step 7

Step 8

Sautéed Ravioli with Spinach and Mushrooms

Expand your pasta repertoire beyond boiling and baking: Try a dish that features sautéed ravioli. Here, the cheese-filled pasta pillows are boiled, then quickly tossed in sizzling butter and oil; the brief browning lightly toasts the ravioli and turns them golden. The ravioli are then served on a bed of velvety stir-fried spinach and mushrooms, nicely setting off the pasta's tempting color and texture.

Working time: 30 minutes
Total time: 30 minutes

Sautéed Ravioli with Spinach and Mushrooms

4 Servings

1 medium onion
½ pound mushrooms
1 pound fresh spinach or 2 packages (10 ounces each) frozen spinach, thawed
3 tablespoons olive or other vegetable oil
4 cloves garlic, minced or crushed through a press

1 pound cheese-filled ravioli
3 tablespoons butter
1½ teaspoons oregano
¼ teaspoon salt
½ teaspoon pepper
¼ cup grated Parmesan cheese

Step 5

1 Bring a large pot of water to a boil.

2 Meanwhile, thinly slice the onion and mushrooms. If using fresh spinach, wash and stem. If using frozen thawed spinach, squeeze out any excess moisture with your hands.

3 In a large skillet, warm 1 tablespoon of the oil over medium-high heat until hot but not smoking. Add the onion and garlic, and cook until the onion begins to soften, 2 to 3 minutes.

4 Add the ravioli to the boiling water and cook until al dente, 8 to 10 minutes, or according to package directions.

5 Meanwhile, add 1 tablespoon of the oil and the mushrooms to the skillet and stir-fry until the mushrooms begin to soften, 3 to 5 minutes.

Step 6

6 Add 2 tablespoons of the butter, the oregano, salt, pepper and spinach, and cook until the spinach is just limp and heated through, about 3 minutes.

7 Divide the spinach and mushrooms among four plates. Drain the ravioli. Add the remaining 1 tablespoon each oil and butter to the skillet. Add the drained ravioli and stir-fry until the ravioli are just beginning to brown, 2 to 3 minutes.

8 Serve the ravioli on top of the spinach and mushrooms. Sprinkle with the Parmesan.

TIME-SAVERS

■ *Do-ahead:* *The vegetables can be prepared ahead of time.*

Step 7

Values are approximate per serving: Calories: 599 Protein: 24 gm Fat: 38 gm
Carbohydrates: 42 gm Cholesterol: 121 mg Sodium: 948 mg

Pasta Salad with Avocado Dressing

▼

The recipe for this simple pasta salad is extremely flexible. If you do not have ham, use 1 cup of cubed cooked turkey or chicken. If you do not have celery, use 1 cup of diced green, yellow or red bell pepper. The rich and creamy avocado dressing is delicious, but if you are counting calories, you may want to substitute plain yogurt for some or all of the mayonnaise.

Working time: 20 minutes
Total time: 20 minutes

Pasta Salad with Avocado Dressing

6 Servings

¼ **pound lean ham, unsliced**
3 **stalks celery**
2 **medium tomatoes**
½ **pound small pasta shells (about 4 cups)**
1 **avocado**

¾ **cup mayonnaise**
2 **tablespoons cider vinegar**
1 **teaspoon Dijon mustard**
½ **teaspoon salt**
¼ **teaspoon pepper**

1 Bring a large pot of water to a boil.

2 Meanwhile, cut the ham, celery and tomatoes into ½-inch cubes.

3 Add the pasta to the boiling water and cook until al dente, 10 to 12 minutes or according to package directions.

4 Meanwhile, make the dressing: In a medium bowl, mash the avocado with a fork. Stir in the mayonnaise, vinegar, mustard, salt and pepper.

5 Drain the pasta, rinse it under cold running water and drain well. Transfer the pasta to a large serving bowl.

6 Add the ham, celery and tomatoes to the pasta and toss gently. Add the dressing and stir gently to evenly coat the ingredients.

TIME-SAVERS

■ *Do-ahead:* *The ham, celery and tomatoes can be prepared ahead. The pasta can be cooked ahead (although you might want to toss it with a small amount of mayonnaise or olive oil so it won't stick together). The avocado dressing can also be made ahead. Although these components can each be assembled ahead of time, it's best to put them together just before serving, to keep the salad from drying out.*

Values are approximate per serving: Calories: 429 Protein: 10 gm Fat: 29 gm
Carbohydrates: 35 gm Cholesterol: 25 mg Sodium: 659 mg

Step 2

Step 4

Step 4

Fettuccine with Mushroom-Spinach Pesto Cream

▼

Spinach, mushrooms, onions, sour cream, basil and Parmesan are combined in this dish to make a velvety green sauce reminiscent of an Italian pesto. Because the quantity of the basil used here is minor compared with the amount called for in a true pesto, dried basil is fine for this recipe. However, if fresh basil is available, use ¼ cup chopped leaves for a fresh, summery taste.

Working time: 20 minutes
Total time: 25 minutes

Fettuccine with Mushroom-Spinach Pesto Cream

4 Servings

1 medium onion
½ pound mushrooms
1 tablespoon olive or other
  vegetable oil
3 cloves garlic, minced or crushed
  through a press
2 tablespoons butter
¾ pound fettuccine

1 package (10 ounces) frozen
  spinach, thawed
1 tablespoon basil
1½ cups sour cream
½ cup grated Parmesan cheese
½ teaspoon salt
¼ teaspoon pepper

Step 4

1 Coarsely chop the onion. Slice the mushrooms.

2 Bring a large pot of water to a boil.

3 In a large skillet, warm the oil over medium-high heat until hot but not smoking. Add the onion and garlic and cook until the mixture is golden, about 5 minutes.

4 Add the butter and warm until melted. Reduce the heat to medium, add the mushrooms and cook until the mushrooms are wilted, about 5 minutes.

5 Add the pasta to the boiling water and cook until al dente, 10 to 12 minutes, or according to package directions.

6 Meanwhile, squeeze the thawed spinach with your hands to remove any excess moisture.

Step 6

7 Add the spinach and basil to the skillet and cook, stirring, until heated through, about 1 minute.

8 Stir in the sour cream, Parmesan, salt and pepper, and cook, stirring, just until heated through, about 1 minute.

9 Drain the pasta and top with the sauce.

TIME-SAVERS

■ *Do-ahead: The sauce can be made ahead through Step 7; before serving, reheat the sauce and stir in the sour cream, Parmesan, salt and pepper.*

Values are approximate per serving: Calories: 680 Protein: 23 gm Fat: 34 gm
Carbohydrates: 73 gm Cholesterol: 142 mg Sodium: 638 mg

Step 8

Angel Hair with Veal, Mushrooms and Peas

▼

Italian-style pasta dishes are not all topped with tomato sauce. This one combines thin strips of veal (a favorite of Italian cooks) with tender mushrooms and green peas; the sauce is simply the pan juices, lightly thickened with a small amount of flour. The veal and vegetables are tossed with angel hair pasta, although any long thin pasta will do just as well.

Working time: 25 minutes
Total time: 25 minutes

Angel Hair with Veal, Mushrooms and Peas

4 Servings

¾ **pound veal cutlets**
1 **medium onion**
½ **pound small mushrooms**
3 **tablespoons flour**
1 **teaspoon oregano**
¼ **teaspoon salt**
¼ **teaspoon pepper**
2 **tablespoons butter**
2 **tablespoons vegetable oil**

½ **pound angel hair or other very thin pasta, such as spaghettini or vermicelli**
2 **cloves garlic, minced or crushed through a press**
1 **cup chicken broth**
1 **cup frozen peas**
¼ **cup grated Parmesan cheese (optional)**

1 Bring a large pot of water to a boil.

2 Meanwhile, cut the veal across the grain into thin strips. Coarsely chop the onion. Halve the mushrooms if they are large.

Step 2

3 In a plastic or paper bag, combine the flour, ½ teaspoon of the oregano, the salt and pepper, and shake to mix. Add the veal and shake to coat lightly. Remove the veal and reserve the excess seasoned flour.

4 In a large skillet, melt 1 tablespoon of the butter in 1 tablespoon of the oil over medium-high heat until hot but not smoking. Add the veal and stir-fry until the meat is evenly browned, about 5 minutes. Remove the veal to a plate and cover loosely to keep warm.

5 Add the pasta to the boiling water and cook until al dente, 10 to 12 minutes, or according to package directions.

Step 4

6 Meanwhile, add the remaining 1 tablespoon butter and 1 tablespoon oil to the skillet and warm over medium-high heat until hot but not smoking. Add the onion and garlic and cook, stirring, until the onion begins to brown, about 5 minutes.

7 Add the mushrooms and cook, stirring, for 1 minute. Add 1 tablespoon of the reserved dredging mixture and stir until the flour is no longer visible.

8 Add the chicken broth, the remaining ½ teaspoon oregano and the peas. Bring to a boil. Return the veal to the skillet and cook, stirring, for 1 minute.

9 Drain the pasta and serve topped with the veal, vegetables and sauce. Accompany with grated Parmesan if desired.

Values are approximate per serving: Calories: 493 Protein: 30 gm Fat: 16 gm
Carbohydrates: 57 gm Cholesterol: 82 mg Sodium: 542 mg

Step 8

Egg Noodles with Cabbage and Paprika

▼

This flavorful side dish makes a satisfying complement to a simple roast beef or chicken dinner. The sautéed onion and cabbage strips, velvety egg noodles and sweet-and-sour sauce create an intriguing blend of flavors and textures. The addition of strips of leftover meat or poultry—ham or chicken breast, for instance—would turn this into a hearty main dish.

Working time: 20 minutes
Total time: 20 minutes

Egg Noodles with Cabbage and Paprika

6 Servings

1 medium onion	½ pound egg noodles
1 pound cabbage (about one-third of a large head)	¼ cup cider vinegar
	1 tablespoon brown sugar
6 tablespoons butter	1 tablespoon paprika
2 tablespoons olive or other vegetable oil	½ teaspoon salt

1 Bring a large pot of water to a boil.

2 Meanwhile, in a food processor with the slicing blade, slice the onion. Remove and set aside. In the same work bowl, shred the cabbage with the slicing blade. Remove and set aside.

Step 2

3 In a large skillet, melt 2 tablespoons of the butter in the oil over medium-high heat until hot but not smoking. Add the onion and stir-fry until it begins to color, about 6 minutes.

4 Add the noodles to the boiling water and cook until al dente, about 9 minutes, or according to package directions.

5 Meanwhile, add the remaining 4 tablespoons butter and the cabbage to the onions in the skillet and cook until the cabbage begins to wilt, about 5 minutes.

6 Add the vinegar, sugar, paprika and salt. Bring the liquid to a boil, reduce the heat to medium-low, cover and simmer until the cabbage is completely wilted, about 1 minute.

7 Drain the pasta and toss it with the cabbage.

Step 5

TIME-SAVERS

■ *Microwave tip: Cook the pasta as directed above. In a 4-quart microwave-safe casserole, melt 4 tablespoons of the butter at 100% for 1 minute. (Omit the remaining 2 tablespoons butter and the oil.) Add the shredded cabbage and onion and toss with the butter. Cover and cook at 100% for 7 minutes, or until the cabbage is crisp-tender. Stir in the vinegar, sugar, paprika and salt; re-cover and cook at 100% for 2 minutes. Toss the cabbage with the cooked pasta.*

■ *Do-ahead: The vegetables can be shredded ahead of time.*

Values are approximate per serving: Calories: 322 Protein: 7 gm Fat: 18 gm
Carbohydrates: 35 gm Cholesterol: 67 mg Sodium: 322 mg

Step 6

Fusilli with Spring Vegetables and Mustard Sauce

Mayonnaise and mustard make an instant creamy "sauce" for this pasta-and-vegetable toss. When it's in season, use fresh asparagus (and fresh peas, if available) in this dish. At other times of the year, you can use frozen asparagus. If you cannot find frozen artichoke hearts, substitute canned or marinated artichoke hearts, but drain, rinse and pat them dry before using.

Working time: 25 minutes
Total time: 25 minutes

Fusilli with Spring Vegetables and Mustard Sauce

6 Servings

½ pound asparagus
2 large carrots
1 medium onion
2 tablespoons olive or other vegetable oil
3 cloves garlic, minced or crushed through a press
½ pound fusilli, or other pasta twists (about 3½ cups)

1 package (10 ounces) frozen artichoke hearts
1 cup frozen peas
⅓ cup mayonnaise
¼ cup grated Parmesan cheese
2 tablespoons Dijon mustard
¼ teaspoon pepper

Step 2

1 Bring a large pot of water to a boil.

2 Meanwhile, cut the asparagus into 2-inch lengths. Cut the carrots into thin slices. Coarsely chop the onion.

3 In a large skillet, warm 1 tablespoon of the oil over medium-high heat until hot but not smoking. Add the onion and garlic and cook until the garlic begins to brown, 2 to 3 minutes.

4 Add the pasta to the boiling water and cook until al dente, 10 to 12 minutes, or according to package directions.

5 Meanwhile, add the remaining 1 tablespoon oil to the skillet and warm over medium-high heat. Add the asparagus, carrots, artichoke hearts and peas, and cook, stirring occasionally, until the carrots and asparagus are tender, 7 to 9 minutes.

Step 5

6 In a large serving bowl, stir together the mayonnaise, Parmesan, mustard and pepper.

7 Drain the pasta. Add the hot pasta and cooked vegetables to the serving bowl and toss well to coat with the sauce.

TIME-SAVERS

■ *Do-ahead: The vegetables can be cut up and the mustard sauce (Step 6) made ahead. The whole dish can be made ahead and served at room temperature or lightly chilled.*

Step 6

Values are approximate per serving: Calories: 354 Protein: 11 gm Fat: 16 gm
Carbohydrates: 43 gm Cholesterol: 10 mg Sodium: 345 mg

Fettuccine with Smoked Salmon and Creamy Dill Sauce

▼

Smoked salmon can be a relatively inexpensive ingredient if you pick up a package from the supermarket dairy case or a rather costly indulgence if you opt for fine imported salmon at a gourmet shop. This recipe requires just four ounces of the savory fish, so either way it won't break your budget. Serve the creamy pasta and salmon with a big tossed salad and crisp breadsticks.

Working time: 20 minutes
Total time: 25 minutes

Fettuccine with Smoked Salmon and Creamy Dill Sauce

4 Servings

1 medium onion
⅓ cup chopped fresh dill or 2½ teaspoons dried
¼ pound smoked salmon
4 tablespoons butter
2 cloves garlic, minced or crushed through a press
¾ pound fettuccine
¼ cup flour

1 cup light cream or half-and-half
½ cup milk
⅓ cup dry white wine or chicken broth
Pinch of nutmeg
½ teaspoon salt
¼ teaspoon pepper, preferably white
⅓ cup grated Parmesan cheese

Step 2

1 Bring a large pot of water to a boil.

2 Meanwhile, coarsely chop the onion and the fresh dill. Cut the salmon into bite-size pieces.

3 In a medium saucepan, warm 2 tablespoons of the butter over medium-high heat until it is melted. Add the onion and garlic, and cook, stirring, until the onion is softened but not browned, about 3 minutes.

4 Add the pasta to the boiling water and cook until al dente, 7 to 9 minutes, or according to package directions.

5 Meanwhile, add the remaining 2 tablespoons butter to the saucepan. Stir in the flour and cook, stirring, until the flour is no longer visible, about 1 minute. Stir in the cream, milk, wine, dill, nutmeg, salt and pepper, and bring to a simmer over medium heat, stirring until smooth. Cook, stirring occasionally, until the sauce is thickened, about 4 minutes.

6 Stir in the salmon and Parmesan.

7 Drain the pasta and serve topped with the sauce.

Step 5

Values are approximate per serving: Calories: 678 Protein: 24 gm Fat: 31 gm
Carbohydrates: 73 gm Cholesterol: 168 mg Sodium: 796 mg

Step 6

Angel Hair Pasta with Green Beans and Almonds

▼

Green beans, olives, almonds and tomatoes provide a wonderful range of colors, tastes and textures for this ultra-simple pasta dish. Using angel hair pasta instead of a thicker pasta shape will cut the cooking time. If you can't find angel hair pasta (also called capellini), try spaghettini; the cooking time should be approximately the same. Of course, spaghetti or linguine will also do nicely.

Working time: 30 minutes
Total time: 30 minutes

Angel Hair Pasta with Green Beans and Almonds

4 Servings

⅓ cup sliced almonds
2 medium onions
2 tablespoons olive oil
2 cloves garlic, minced or crushed
    through a press
½ pound fresh green beans or
    1½ cups frozen, thawed

1 cup pitted black olives (optional)
½ pound angel hair pasta
    (capellini) or spaghettini
1 can (14 ounces) whole tomatoes,
    drained
3 tablespoons chopped parsley
    (optional)

Step 3

1 Bring a large pot of water to a boil.

2 Meanwhile, toast the almonds: In an ungreased skillet, sauté the almonds over medium heat, shaking the pan frequently, until lightly browned, about 3 minutes. Or, place the almonds in the tray of a toaster oven set to 375° and toast until lightly browned, 3 to 4 minutes. Set aside.

3 Halve and slice the onions. In a large skillet, warm the oil over medium-high heat. Add the onions and garlic and sauté until the onions are well browned, about 10 minutes.

4 Cut the fresh green beans into 2-inch lengths. Halve the olives (if using). Add the green beans and olives to the skillet and stir-fry for 3 minutes.

Step 6

5 Add the pasta to the boiling water and cook until al dente, about 5 minutes or according to the package directions.

6 Meanwhile, add the tomatoes to the skillet, breaking them up with a spoon, and cook the mixture for another 2 minutes. Add the parsley (if using) and cook for 1 minute longer. Remove from the heat.

7 Drain the pasta well and place in a large serving bowl. Add the green bean and tomato mixture and toss well to combine.

8 Divide the pasta among 4 plates and sprinkle with the reserved toasted almonds.

TIME-SAVERS

■ *Do-ahead: The almonds can be toasted ahead of time. To save time, the almonds can also be used untoasted or omitted altogether. The sauce can be made (through Step 6) ahead of time and reheated gently on the stovetop or in the microwave.*

Step 7

Values are approximate per serving: Calories: 368   Protein: 11 gm   Fat: 12 gm
Carbohydrates: 56 gm   Cholesterol: 0 mg   Sodium: 168 mg

Lemon Fettuccine with Artichokes

Marinated artichoke hearts, which come in handy for dressing up salads and appetizers, should be on every cook's "emergency shelf" of packaged foods. Here, two jars of artichokes are tossed with fettuccine, while the liquid from one jar is used in the sauce. Lots of lemon flavors this dish as well—a quartered lemon goes into the pasta water, and the fettuccine and sauce are tossed with lemon zest and juice just before serving.

Working time: 15 minutes
Total time: 15 minutes

4 Servings

2 lemons
1 medium onion
1 pound part-skim mozzarella
1 tablespoon olive or other
  vegetable oil
2 cloves garlic, minced or crushed
  through a press

½ pound egg fettuccine
2 jars (6 ounces each) marinated
  artichoke hearts
1 cup sour cream
¼ cup chopped parsley (optional)

1 Bring a large pot of water to a boil. Quarter one of the lemons and add it to the pot.

2 Meanwhile, finely grate the zest of the remaining lemon and then juice the lemon. Coarsely chop the onion. Cut the mozzarella into ½-inch cubes.

Step 2

3 In a medium skillet, warm the oil over medium-high heat until hot but not smoking. Add the onion and garlic and stir-fry until the mixture begins to brown, about 5 minutes.

4 Add the pasta to the boiling water and cook until al dente, 4 to 5 minutes, or according to package directions.

5 Meanwhile, drain one of the jars of artichokes. Add the drained artichokes and the second jar of artichokes with its liquid to the skillet. Cook, stirring frequently, until the artichokes are heated through, about 3 minutes.

6 Stir the sour cream and mozzarella into the skillet and remove from the heat.

Step 5

7 Drain the pasta and discard the lemon quarters. Toss the pasta with the artichoke mixture, lemon juice, lemon zest and parsley (if using).

TIME-SAVERS

■ ***Do-ahead:*** *The ingredients can all be prepared ahead and the sauce can be made ahead through Step 5. Cook the pasta and finish the sauce just before serving.*

Values are approximate per serving: Calories: 720 Protein: 39 gm Fat: 39 gm
Carbohydrates: 54 gm Cholesterol: 145 mg Sodium: 804 mg

Step 6

Spaghetti Primavera with Chicken

▼

Strictly speaking, an Italian pasta "primavera" would be made with young spring vegetables—primavera means spring—but this adaptation uses mushrooms, scallions and bell pepper, which are available all year long. For a change of pace, substitute oregano or basil (either dried or, if available, fresh minced) for the dill.

Working time: 20 minutes
Total time: 20 minutes

4 Servings

¾ **pound skinless, boneless chicken breast**
½ **pound mushrooms**
1 **medium yellow or green bell pepper**
1 **bunch scallions (6 to 8)**
½ **pound spaghetti**
5 **tablespoons light olive or other vegetable oil**

2 **cloves garlic, minced or crushed through a press**
¼ **cup chopped fresh dill or 1 teaspoon dried**
¾ **teaspoon salt**
¼ **teaspoon black pepper**

1 Bring a large pot of water to a boil.

2 Meanwhile, cut the chicken into 1-inch cubes. Cut the mushrooms into ¼-inch-thick slices. Cut the bell pepper into slivers. Coarsely chop the scallions.

3 Add the spaghetti to the boiling water and cook until al dente, 10 to 12 minutes or according to package directions.

4 Meanwhile, in a large skillet or flameproof casserole, warm 2 tablespoons of the oil over medium-high heat until hot but not smoking. Add the chicken and sauté until the chicken turns white, 2 to 3 minutes.

Step 4

5 Add the mushrooms, bell pepper, scallions, garlic and remaining 3 tablespoons oil and sauté until the vegetables are softened but not browned, 2 to 3 minutes.

6 Drain the spaghetti and add it to the skillet, along with the dill, salt and black pepper. Gently toss the ingredients together and serve hot.

Step 5

TIME-SAVERS

■ ***Do-ahead:*** *The chicken, mushrooms, bell pepper and scallions can be cut up ahead of time.*

Values are approximate per serving: Calories: 481   Protein: 29 gm   Fat: 19 gm
Carbohydrates: 48 gm   Cholesterol: 49 mg   Sodium: 473 mg

Step 6

Fettuccine with Sole and Yellow Squash in Cream

This delicate-looking pasta dish is a superb springtime entrée—and a
perfect excuse for an impromptu dinner party, as you can easily put it together
after work. The fish and vegetables take only minutes to cut up,
after which they are sautéed very briefly while the pasta cooks. Heavy
cream added to the skillet forms a delectable sauce.

Working time: 20 minutes
Total time: 25 minutes

Fettuccine with Sole and Yellow Squash in Cream

4 Servings

4 scallions
¼ cup fresh dill sprigs or 1 tablespoon dried dill
2 large yellow squash (about 1 pound)
1 pound fillet of sole or other firm-fleshed white fish
½ pound fettuccine

1 tablespoon butter
1 tablespoon olive or other vegetable oil
2 cloves garlic, minced or crushed through a press
½ cup heavy cream
½ teaspoon salt
¼ teaspoon pepper

Step 2

1 Bring a large pot of water to a boil.

2 Meanwhile, coarsely chop the scallions. Finely chop the dill. Halve the squash lengthwise and then cut crosswise into ¼-inch half-rounds. Cut the sole into 1-inch pieces.

3 Add the pasta to the boiling water and cook until al dente, 10 to 12 minutes, or according to package directions.

4 Meanwhile, in a large skillet, warm the butter in the oil over medium-high heat until the butter is melted. Add the scallions and garlic and cook, stirring, until the scallions are wilted, about 3 minutes.

5 Add the dill and squash and cook, stirring, until the squash begins to wilt, about 3 minutes.

Step 2

6 Add the sole, cream, salt and pepper, and let the mixture come to a boil, stirring gently so as not to break up the fish. Cook until the fish just flakes when tested with a fork, about 3 minutes.

7 Drain the pasta and serve it topped with the sauce.

TIME-SAVERS

■ *Microwave tip: Cook the pasta as directed above. Meanwhile, in a shallow microwave-safe baking dish, combine the butter, oil, scallions, garlic, only 2 tablespoons of fresh dill (or 1½ teaspoons dried), the squash, cream, salt and pepper. Cover and cook at 100% for 5 minutes. Add the fish, re-cover and cook at 100% for 5 minutes, or until the fish is done and vegetables are just tender.*

■ *Do-ahead: The vegetables and fish can be cut up ahead.*

Values are approximate per serving: Calories: 313 Protein: 24 gm Fat: 19 gm
Carbohydrates: 11 gm Cholesterol: 108 mg Sodium: 412 mg

Step 6

Spinach Soup with Ravioli and Parmesan Toasts

▼

The basil-scented broth for this highly satisfying soup is filled with plump cheese ravioli, julienned carrots, tender spinach leaves and stir-fried red onions. The soup is topped with crisp, golden cheese croutons. If you do not have fresh spinach on hand, use half of a 10-ounce package of frozen leaf (not chopped) spinach. Thaw it, drain it well on paper towels and add it to the soup just before serving.

Working time: 25 minutes
Total time: 30 minutes

Spinach Soup with Ravioli and Parmesan Toasts

4 Servings

2 medium carrots
1 medium red onion
1 tablespoon plus 2 teaspoons olive
  or other vegetable oil
2 cloves garlic, minced or crushed
  through a press
2 cups chicken broth
2 cups water

1 teaspoon basil
¼ teaspoon black pepper
Pinch of red pepper flakes
2 slices firm-textured white bread
2 tablespoons grated Parmesan
  cheese
1 pound cheese-filled ravioli
¼ pound fresh spinach

Step 1

1 Cut the carrots into 2-inch-long matchsticks. Cut the onion into thin wedges.

2 In a large saucepan, warm 1 tablespoon of the oil over medium-high heat until hot but not smoking. Add the onion and garlic, and stir-fry until the onion begins to brown, about 5 minutes.

3 Add the carrots, chicken broth, water, basil, black pepper and red pepper flakes, and bring the mixture to a boil.

4 Meanwhile, sprinkle the bread with the Parmesan and drizzle on the remaining 2 teaspoons oil. Toast under the broiler or in a toaster oven until golden, about 2 minutes. Cut each slice into 8 triangles.

Step 4

5 When the broth has come to a boil, add the ravioli and cook, uncovered, until the ravioli are cooked through, 9 minutes or according to package directions.

6 Meanwhile, stem the spinach and tear it into large pieces. One minute before the ravioli are done, add the spinach. Stir to wilt the spinach and remove from the heat.

7 Serve the soup topped with the Parmesan toasts.

TIME-SAVERS

■ *Do-ahead: The soup can be prepared ahead through Step 3.*

Step 6

Values are approximate per serving: Calories: 503 Protein: 22 gm Fat: 25 gm
Carbohydrates: 47 gm Cholesterol: 96 mg Sodium: 966 mg

Chicken and Tiny Star Pasta Stew (page 91)

CHAPTER 2
POULTRY

Devilish Drumsticks with Cheese Sauce

▼

*The spicy favorite Buffalo Wings, which were first created in a Buffalo,
New York, restaurant, provided the inspiration for this recipe. Here, broiled
drumsticks (which offer more meat per serving) are used instead of
deep-fried chicken wings, and herbs, cream cheese and yogurt replace the traditional
blue cheese sauce. If desired, serve more hot sauce on the side.*

Working time: 10 minutes
Total time: 30 minutes

Devilish Drumsticks with Cheese Sauce

4 Servings

1 package (3 ounces) cream cheese, at room temperature
¼ cup plain yogurt
2 tablespoons chopped parsley (optional)
1 clove garlic, minced or crushed through a press

½ teaspoon oregano
¼ teaspoon salt
¼ teaspoon pepper
3 tablespoons butter
3 tablespoons hot pepper sauce
8 chicken drumsticks (about 1¾ pounds total)

1 Preheat the broiler. Line a broiler pan with foil.

2 In a small bowl, beat together the softened cream cheese, yogurt, parsley (if using), garlic, oregano, salt and pepper. Cover the bowl and refrigerate until serving time.

Step 2

3 Melt the butter in the microwave or on the stovetop. Stir the hot sauce into the melted butter.

4 Dip each drumstick into the butter mixture until completely coated and place them on the foil-lined pan. Broil the drumsticks 4 inches from the heat, about 7 minutes per side, or until the skin is golden and the juices run clear when pierced with a knife.

5 Serve the drumsticks with the cream cheese-yogurt sauce on the side.

Step 3

TIME-SAVERS

■ **Microwave tip:** *To soften the cream cheese, remove it from its wrapper and place it in a small microwave-safe bowl and microwave at 50% for about 45 seconds. Mix the remaining cheese sauce ingredients directly into the softened cream cheese. Also, the butter can be melted in the microwave: Place the butter in a microwave-safe bowl and cook at 100% for 30 seconds, then stir in the hot sauce.*

■ **Do-ahead:** *The cheese sauce (Step 2) can be made ahead. The whole dish can be made ahead and served at room temperature.*

Step 4

Values are approximate per serving: Calories: 339 Protein: 26 gm Fat: 25 gm
Carbohydrates: 2 gm Cholesterol: 123 mg Sodium: 605 mg

Chicken Breasts with Apricots and Almonds

This dish captures the flavors of an Indian biryani, an aromatic mingling of meat, spices, dried fruit and nuts. Because rice is also a main component of a biryani, it would be the perfect accompaniment here. Try this recipe even if you're not a curry fan, as the curry flavor is quite subtle. The almonds will taste better if you toast them, but you can skip this step if you're short on time.

Working time: 15 minutes
Total time: 25 minutes

Chicken Breasts with Apricots and Almonds

4 Servings

3 tablespoons flour
2 teaspoons curry powder
½ teaspoon salt
¼ teaspoon pepper
4 skinless, boneless chicken breast
  halves (about 1¼ pounds total)
1 tablespoon butter
1 tablespoon olive oil

1 cup chicken broth
2 tablespoons tomato paste
½ cup golden or regular raisins
½ teaspoon sugar
½ cup dried apricots
¼ cup sliced almonds
2 scallions

1 In a plastic or paper bag, combine the flour, 1 teaspoon of the curry powder, the salt and pepper, and shake to mix. Add the chicken and shake to coat lightly. Remove the chicken and reserve the excess seasoned flour.

2 In a large skillet, warm the butter in the oil over medium-high heat until the butter melts. Add the chicken and brown all over, about 5 minutes per side. Remove to a plate and cover loosely to keep warm.

3 Add 1 tablespoon of the reserved dredging mixture to the skillet and cook, stirring, over medium heat, until the flour is no longer visible, about 1 minute.

4 Stir in the chicken broth, tomato paste, raisins, remaining 1 teaspoon curry powder and the sugar. Bring the mixture to a boil over medium-high heat.

5 Meanwhile, coarsely chop the apricots.

6 When the mixture has come to a boil, stir in the apricots. Return the chicken (and any juices that have accumulated on the plate) to the skillet. Reduce the heat to medium-low, cover and simmer until the chicken is cooked through, about 5 minutes longer, turning once.

7 Meanwhile, toast the almonds for 5 minutes in a 375° oven or toaster oven, watching carefully. Coarsely chop the scallions.

8 Before serving, stir the scallions into the skillet. Serve the chicken topped with sauce and sprinkled with toasted almonds.

TIME-SAVERS

■ *Microwave tip: To toast the almonds, place them in a single layer in a pie plate and drizzle with 1 teaspoon of oil. Cook at 100% for 5 minutes, or until golden brown, stirring once.*

Values are approximate per serving: Calories: 411 Protein: 37 gm Fat: 12 gm
Carbohydrates: 41 gm Cholesterol: 90 mg Sodium: 713 mg

Step 2

Step 4

Step 6

French Potato-Chicken Salad

▼

When making potato salad, choose waxy boiling potatoes. Two familiar types are the round "Red Bliss" and the tapered tan "White Rose." These varieties hold their shape when cut up and cooked, making for a more attractive salad. You can also make this salad with leftovers or deli meats: use a half-pound of ham, chicken, or smoked or regular turkey.

Working time: 10 minutes
Total time: 30 minutes

6 Servings

1 pound boiling potatoes, unpeeled
½ pound fresh green beans or
   1 package (10 ounces) frozen
   green beans, thawed
2 skinless, boneless chicken breast
   halves (about ½ pound total)
¼ cup olive or other vegetable oil
2 tablespoons white wine vinegar
   or cider vinegar

1 tablespoon Dijon mustard
¾ teaspoon Worcestershire sauce
2 tablespoons minced fresh dill or
   2 teaspoons dried
¼ teaspoon salt
Pinch of pepper

Step 1

1 Cut the potatoes into ½-inch chunks. Steam the potatoes in a steamer for 10 minutes.

2 Meanwhile, cut the beans into 2-inch lengths. Add the beans to the steamer, cover and cook until the potatoes are just tender and the beans are crisp-tender, 5 to 8 minutes longer.

3 Meanwhile, cut the chicken into bite-size pieces. Remove the vegetables from the steamer and set aside. Place the chicken in the steamer, cover and cook until opaque throughout, about 6 minutes.

4 In a small bowl, combine the oil, vinegar, mustard, Worcestershire sauce, dill, salt and pepper.

5 Place the potatoes, green beans and chicken in a serving bowl, add the dressing and toss to combine well. Serve the salad warm or at room temperature.

Step 2

TIME-SAVERS

■ *Do-ahead: The individual components can be steamed ahead. Or, the whole salad can be assembled ahead and served at room temperature or chilled.*

Values are approximate per serving: Calories: 199 Protein: 11 gm Fat: 10 gm
Carbohydrates: 17 gm Cholesterol: 22 mg Sodium: 205 mg

Step 5

Lime-Grilled Turkey Cutlet Sandwiches

▼

A lime-juice marinade gives a burst of fresh flavor to the broiled turkey cutlets in these California-style sandwiches. Lime mayonnaise is the complementary spread, and avocado slices and a spoonful of cranberry sauce for zip are the finishing touches. For best flavor, toast the rolls under the broiler for a moment, and serve the sandwiches soon after they are assembled.

Working time: 20 minutes
Total time: 20 minutes

Lime-Grilled Turkey Cutlet Sandwiches

4 Servings

4 turkey cutlets (¼ inch thick, about ½ pound total)
¼ cup lime juice
1 tablespoon olive or other vegetable oil
½ teaspoon salt
¼ teaspoon pepper
⅓ cup mayonnaise

2 tablespoons chopped cilantro (optional)
1 teaspoon grated lime zest (optional)
½ avocado
4 club rolls or other hard rolls
4 lettuce leaves
¼ cup cranberry sauce

Step 2

1 Preheat the broiler. Line a broiler pan with foil and lightly grease the foil.

2 Place the turkey cutlets in a shallow dish and sprinkle them with 2 tablespoons of the lime juice, the olive oil, salt and pepper. Turn the cutlets to coat them thoroughly with the seasonings.

3 Place the turkey cutlets on the prepared broiler pan and broil them 4 inches from the heat for 3 minutes per side.

4 Meanwhile, in a small bowl, stir together 1 tablespoon of the lime juice, the mayonnaise, and the cilantro and lime zest (if using).

5 Slice the avocado and toss it with the remaining 1 tablespoon lime juice.

Step 5

6 Split the rolls lengthwise and place them cut-side up under the broiler for about 30 seconds, or until lightly toasted.

7 Spread both halves of each roll with the lime mayonnaise. Place a lettuce leaf and a turkey cutlet on half of each roll and top with avocado slices and a spoonful of cranberry sauce.

TIME-SAVERS

■ *Do-ahead: The turkey can be marinated and even broiled ahead. The lime mayonnaise (Step 4) can be made ahead; cover and refrigerate.*

Values are approximate per serving: Calories: 451 Protein: 19 gm Fat: 24 gm
Carbohydrates: 40 gm Cholesterol: 47 mg Sodium: 738 mg

Step 7

Chicken-Vegetable Stir-Fry with Walnuts

▼

As with nearly any stir-fry, all you need to add to this main course to make a complete meal is some steamed white rice—which will cook in the same amount of time it takes to prepare the stir-fry. If you are concerned about your sodium intake, you can reduce the levels in this recipe by using one of the "lite" soy sauces now available. Or take ordinary soy sauce and dilute it by one-third with some water or chicken broth.

Working time: 30 minutes
Total time: 30 minutes

Chicken-Vegetable Stir-Fry with Walnuts

4 Servings

2 skinless, boneless chicken breast halves (about 10 ounces)
3 tablespoons vegetable oil
2 tablespoons reduced-sodium or regular soy sauce
1½ tablespoons cornstarch
1 large red bell pepper
1 medium red onion
1 large stalk broccoli

¾ cup chicken broth
½ teaspoon sugar
¼ teaspoon dried red pepper flakes
2 cloves garlic, crushed through a press
1 can (8 ounces) sliced water chestnuts, drained
¼ cup walnut halves or pieces

Step 1

1 Cut the chicken into 1-inch cubes. Place the chicken in a bowl and add 1 tablespoon of the oil, 1 tablespoon of the soy sauce and 1 tablespoon of the cornstarch. Toss to thoroughly coat the chicken.

2 Cut the bell pepper into 1-inch squares. Halve the onion and cut it into ¼-inch-thick slices. Separate the broccoli florets from the stem and cut the stem into ¼-inch-thick slices.

3 In a small bowl, combine the broth, sugar, red pepper flakes and the remaining 1 tablespoon soy sauce and 1½ teaspoons cornstarch.

4 In a large skillet or wok, warm 1 tablespoon of the oil over medium-high heat. When the oil is very hot but not smoking, add the chicken and the marinade and stir-fry for 2 to 3 minutes, or until the chicken is opaque but still slightly pink in the center. Transfer the chicken to a plate and set aside.

Step 5

5 Add the remaining 1 tablespoon oil to the skillet. Add the bell pepper, onion, broccoli, garlic and water chestnuts and stir-fry until the onions begin to wilt, 2 to 3 minutes.

6 Return the chicken to the skillet and add the walnuts. Stir the broth mixture, add it to the skillet and bring the liquid to a boil.

7 Cook, stirring constantly, until the vegetables are crisp-tender and the chicken is cooked through, 2 to 3 minutes longer. Serve hot.

TIME-SAVERS

■ *Do-ahead: The chicken can be cut up and tossed with its marinade (Step 1) ahead of time. The bell pepper, onion and broccoli can be prepared ahead. The seasoned broth (Step 3) can be made ahead.*

Step 6

Values are approximate per serving: Calories: 295 Protein: 22 gm Fat: 16 gm
Carbohydrates: 18 gm Cholesterol: 44 mg Sodium: 555 mg

Chicken Tortilla Soup

In most chicken soups, the morsels of chicken are usually quite bland, having had the flavor cooked out of them to make the broth. Not so with this soup, in which the chicken is intensely flavorful. The secret lies in broiling chicken separately, then adding it to the soup just before serving. Toasted tortilla strips give the soup body; chopped jalapeño and shredded Monterey jack cheese add more Mexican flavor.

Working time: 25 minutes
Total time: 30 minutes

Chicken Tortilla Soup

4 Servings

3 cloves garlic
1 medium onion
⅓ cup (packed) cilantro leaves
1 tablespoon plus 2 teaspoons oil
2 teaspoons cumin
1½ teaspoons oregano
½ teaspoon black pepper
½ pound skinless, boneless chicken
   breast
2 cups chicken broth
1 cup water

1 can (14½ ounces) stewed
   tomatoes, with their juice
1 cup tomato juice
2 tablespoons lime juice
½ teaspoon Worcestershire sauce
2 teaspoons grated lime zest
   (optional)
4 corn tortillas (5½-inch diameter)
1 fresh or pickled jalapeño pepper
½ cup shredded Monterey jack
   cheese (about 2 ounces)

Step 4

1 Preheat the broiler. Line a broiler pan with foil.

2 In a food processor, mince the garlic. Add the onion and coarsely chop; remove and set aside. In the same processor work bowl, finely chop the cilantro.

3 In a small bowl, combine half the garlic-onion mixture, half the cilantro, 1 tablespoon of the oil, 1 teaspoon of the cumin, ½ teaspoon of the oregano and ¼ teaspoon of the black pepper.

4 Place the chicken on the broiler pan and spoon the onion-herb mixture on top. Broil 4 inches from the heat for 7 minutes. Turn the chicken over, baste with any pan juices and broil until cooked through, about 7 minutes longer. Remove the chicken to a plate to cool slightly. Set the oven temperature to 400°.

5 Meanwhile, in a medium saucepan, warm the remaining 2 teaspoons oil over medium-high heat. Add the remaining garlic-onion mixture and stir-fry until the onion begins to brown, 3 to 4 minutes.

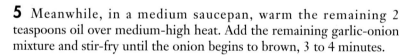
Step 6

6 Add the chicken broth, water, stewed tomatoes and their juice, tomato juice, lime juice, Worcestershire sauce, lime zest (if using), remaining cilantro, 1 teaspoon cumin, 1 teaspoon oregano and ¼ teaspoon black pepper. Bring the mixture to a boil; reduce the heat to low, cover and simmer while you prepare the remaining ingredients.

7 Halve the tortillas, then cut crosswise into strips. Place on a baking sheet and place in the 400° oven to toast them, about 7 minutes.

8 Meanwhile, seed and mince the jalapeño, then stir it into the simmering soup. Shred the cheese. Shred the chicken. To serve, ladle the soup into bowls. Top with chicken slices, tortilla strips and cheese.

Values are approximate per serving: Calories: 343 Protein: 22 gm Fat: 17 gm
Carbohydrates: 27 gm Cholesterol: 45 mg Sodium: 1151 mg

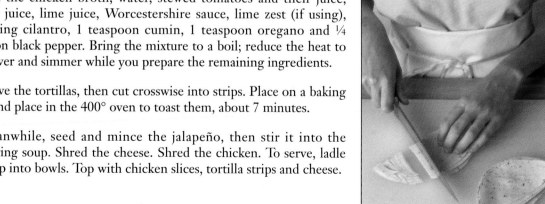
Step 7

Broiled Chicken
with Cheddar-Dill Sauce

▼

You can buy bottled cheese sauce, process cheese or cheese spreads, but there's nothing like a rich homemade Cheddar sauce for velvety texture and full flavor. This smooth Cheddar-dill topping is made like a basic white sauce, with butter, flour and milk. You bring the mixture to a boil before adding the cheese, but be sure to remove the pan from the heat as soon as the cheese is melted; the sauce may become rubbery if overheated.

Working time: 20 minutes
Total time: 25 minutes

4 Servings

1½ tablespoons chopped fresh dill or 1 teaspoon dried	4 skinless, boneless chicken breast halves (about 1¼ pounds total)
½ cup chopped chives or scallion greens	1½ tablespoons flour
3 tablespoons butter	½ cup milk
2 cloves garlic, minced or crushed through a press	½ cup grated Cheddar cheese
¼ teaspoon black pepper	Pinch of salt
	Pinch of pepper, preferably white

Step 2

1 Preheat the broiler. Line a broiler pan with foil.

2 Mince the dill and set aside. Finely chop the chives (or scallion greens).

3 In a small saucepan or skillet, melt 2 tablespoons of the butter. Add half the chives, the garlic and black pepper.

4 Place the chicken on the broiler pan and brush with half the herbed butter. Broil 4 inches from the heat for 7 minutes. Turn the chicken over, brush with the remaining herbed butter and broil for 7 minutes, or until the chicken is cooked through.

Step 4

5 Meanwhile, in a small saucepan, melt the remaining 1 tablespoon butter over medium heat. Stir in the flour and cook, stirring, until the flour is no longer visible, about 30 seconds. Gradually stir in the milk and cook, stirring, until smooth. Bring the mixture to a boil over medium heat.

6 Reduce the heat to medium-low and stir in the Cheddar, dill, remaining chives, salt and white pepper. Stir until the cheese is melted and remove from the heat. When the chicken is done, add any juices that have accumulated on the broiler pan to the cheese sauce.

7 Serve the chicken topped with the sauce.

TIME-SAVERS

■ *Microwave tip:* *To make the sauce, place the butter in a medium bowl and cook at 100% for 30 seconds, or until melted. Stir in the flour. Gradually stir in the milk. Cook at 50% for 2 minutes, or until the milk is hot. Stir in the Cheddar, dill, chives, salt and pepper, stirring until smooth. Reheat at 50% for 1 minute, if necessary.*

Values are approximate per serving: Calories: 338 Protein: 37 gm Fat: 18 gm
Carbohydrates: 5 gm Cholesterol: 130 mg Sodium: 301 mg

Step 6

Ginger-Scallion Chicken with Oriental Salad

▼

This recipe boasts a timesaving two-for-one technique: Minced ginger, garlic and scallions are combined with sesame oil and the resulting paste does double-duty as a flavoring for the chicken and as a salad dressing seasoning. The paste is rubbed all over the chicken, even under the skin (a trick you can use with any spice paste). While the chicken broils, you put together a simple salad of sprouts, carrots and snow peas.

Working time: 20 minutes
Total time: 30 minutes

Ginger-Scallion Chicken with Oriental Salad

4 Servings

6 quarter-size slices (¼ inch thick) fresh ginger, unpeeled
4 cloves garlic
3 scallions
4 tablespoons Oriental sesame oil
1¼ teaspoons salt
¾ teaspoon black pepper
4 chicken breast halves, with skin (about 2 pounds total)
2 medium carrots
¼ pound snow peas

2 cups bean sprouts (about ¼ pound)
3 tablespoons chopped cilantro (optional)
1 tablespoon lemon juice
1 teaspoon grated lemon zest (optional)
¼ teaspoon red pepper flakes
Pinch of sugar
1 tablespoon sesame seeds

1 Preheat the broiler. Line a broiler pan with foil.

2 In a food processor, mince the ginger, garlic and scallions.

3 Transfer the ginger-scallion mixture to a small bowl and add 2 tablespoons of the sesame oil, ¾ teaspoon of the salt and ½ teaspoon of the black pepper. Set aside 1 teaspoon of the mixture.

Step 4

4 Use the remainder of the mixture to coat the chicken: Smear one-third of the mixture under the skin and one-third of it on the skin. Place the chicken skin-side down on the broiler pan and rub the remaining ginger-scallion mixture on the bone side. Broil the chicken 4 inches from the heat for 9 minutes. Turn the chicken over and broil for 9 minutes, or until cooked through.

5 Meanwhile, in the same processor work bowl, coarsely chop the carrots. By hand, cut the snow peas into thin strips. In a medium bowl, combine the carrots, snow peas and bean sprouts.

6 In a small bowl, combine the reserved 1 teaspoon ginger-scallion mixture with the cilantro (if using), lemon juice, lemon zest (if using), red pepper flakes, sugar and remaining 2 tablespoons sesame oil, ½ teaspoon salt and ¼ teaspoon black pepper.

Step 5

7 Pour the dressing over the salad and toss to combine. Serve the salad with the hot chicken and sprinkle both with sesame seeds.

TIME-SAVERS

■ ***Do-ahead:*** *The ginger-scallion mixture (Steps 2 and 3) and the salad dressing (Steps 2, 3 and 6) can be made ahead. The salad vegetables can be cut up a short time ahead.*

Values are approximate per serving: Calories: 423 Protein: 39 gm Fat: 24 gm
Carbohydrates: 11 gm Cholesterol: 103 mg Sodium: 790 mg

Step 7

Honey-Thyme Turkey with Lemon Noodles

▼

A honey-butter baste, flavored with thyme, gives these broiled turkey cutlets a golden-brown finish. Although honey is a common pantry item—it will keep almost indefinitely—when it sits for a long enough time it will crystallize. To solve this problem, heat the open jar in a pan of water, or cover it with plastic wrap and microwave it for 45 seconds to 1½ minutes, depending on how full the jar is.

Working time: 15 minutes
Total time: 25 minutes

Honey-Thyme Turkey with Lemon Noodles

4 Servings

2 tablespoons plus 1 teaspoon butter
2 tablespoons honey
1 teaspoon thyme
¾ teaspoon salt
½ teaspoon pepper
¾ pound wide egg noodles

4 turkey cutlets (about 1 pound total)
3 scallions
3 tablespoons lemon juice
1½ teaspoons grated lemon zest (optional)

1 Bring a large pot of water to a boil. Preheat the broiler. Line a broiler pan with foil and lightly grease the foil.

2 Meanwhile, in a small skillet or saucepan, combine 2 tablespoons of the butter with the honey, thyme and ¼ teaspoon each salt and pepper, and cook over low heat until the butter is melted, about 6 minutes.

3 Add the noodles to the boiling water and cook until al dente, 8 to 10 minutes, or according to package directions.

4 Place the turkey cutlets on the broiler pan. Brush them with half the honey-butter mixture and broil 4 inches from the heat until lightly browned, about 4 minutes.

5 Turn the cutlets over, brush with the remaining honey-butter mixture and broil until cooked through, about 3 minutes.

6 Meanwhile, chop the scallions.

7 Drain the noodles and toss with the scallions, the remaining 1 teaspoon butter, ½ teaspoon salt, ¼ teaspoon pepper, the lemon juice, lemon zest (if using) and any juices from the broiler pan. Serve the noodles alongside the turkey.

TIME-SAVERS

■ *Microwave tip: To make the honey-butter mixture (Step 2), combine the 2 tablespoons butter, the honey, thyme and ¼ teaspoon each salt and pepper in a small microwave-safe bowl and cook at 100% until melted, about 1½ minutes.*

■ *Do-ahead: The honey-butter mixture can be made ahead.*

Values are approximate per serving: Calories: 552 Protein: 39 gm Fat: 12 gm
Carbohydrates: 71 gm Cholesterol: 169 mg Sodium: 578 mg

Step 2

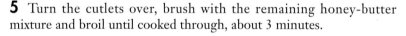
Step 4

Step 7

Curried Chicken and Peas

Introduce your family to the flavors of India with this easy dish. The only accompaniment needed is white rice, which can cook in the time it takes to make the curry. If you prefer, instead of cooking the raisins in the sauce, you can serve them on the side for sprinkling on top of the curry. Other condiments that go well with curry are diced apple and slivered almonds.

Working time: 25 minutes
Total time: 30 minutes

Curried Chicken and Peas

4 Servings

5 scallions
3 tablespoons cornstarch
¼ teaspoon salt
¼ teaspoon pepper
4 skinless, boneless chicken breast
   halves (about 1¼ pounds total)
3 tablespoons olive or other
   vegetable oil

2 cloves garlic, minced or crushed
   through a press
1¼ cups chicken broth
2 tablespoons curry powder
1 teaspoon basil
½ cup golden raisins (optional)
1 cup frozen peas

Step 2

1 Coarsely chop the scallions.

2 In a shallow bowl, combine the cornstarch, salt and pepper. Dredge the chicken breasts in the seasoned cornstarch. Reserve the excess cornstarch mixture.

3 In a large skillet, warm 1 tablespoon of the oil over medium-high heat until hot but not smoking. Add the scallions and garlic and sauté until the scallions begin to wilt, about 2 minutes.

4 Add the remaining 2 tablespoons oil to the skillet, add the chicken breasts and cook until golden all over, 2 to 3 minutes per side.

5 Stir the chicken broth into the reserved cornstarch mixture.

6 Add the broth mixture to the skillet. Add the curry powder, basil and raisins (if using). Bring the liquid to a boil, reduce the heat to medium-low, cover and simmer for 5 minutes.

7 Uncover the skillet and increase the heat to medium-high. Turn the chicken over, add the peas and cook, stirring, for 5 minutes longer.

Step 5

Step 6

Values are approximate per serving: Calories: 323 Protein: 37 gm Fat: 13 gm
Carbohydrates: 14 gm Cholesterol: 82 mg Sodium: 579 mg

Turkey Breast with Tomato-Horseradish Sauce

▼

The tomato sauce that accompanies these sautéed turkey cutlets gets its kick from horseradish. Depending on the strength of your horseradish (bottled horseradish will lose its heat over time), add from two to four tablespoons to the sauce. And if you have access to whole horseradish root, try the sauce with freshly grated; but cut the quantity by at least half, as fresh horseradish is hot enough to bring tears to your eyes.

Working time: 20 minutes
Total time: 30 minutes

Turkey Breast with Tomato-Horseradish Sauce

4 Servings

⅓ cup flour
½ teaspoon black pepper
1 egg white
4 turkey cutlets (about 1 pound total)
2 tablespoons butter
2 tablespoons olive or other vegetable oil
3 cloves garlic
1 medium onion
2 ribs celery
1 medium green bell pepper
1 cup canned whole tomatoes, with their juice
3 tablespoons drained prepared horseradish
¾ teaspoon basil
½ teaspoon sugar
½ teaspoon salt
Pinch of cayenne pepper

Step 2

1 In a shallow bowl, combine the flour and black pepper. In another shallow bowl, lightly beat the egg white.

2 Dip the turkey cutlets in the egg white, then lightly dredge them in the seasoned flour. Reserve any excess flour mixture.

3 In a large skillet, warm 1 tablespoon of the butter in 1 tablespoon of the oil over medium-high heat until the butter is melted. Add the turkey and cook until golden on both sides, about 6 minutes. Remove the turkey to a plate and cover loosely to keep warm.

4 Meanwhile, in a food processor, mince the garlic. Add the onion and coarsely chop; remove and set aside. In the same work bowl, coarsely chop the celery and bell pepper together; remove and set aside.

Step 6

5 Add the remaining 1 tablespoon oil to the skillet. Add the garlic-onion mixture and stir-fry until the onion begins to brown, about 5 minutes.

6 Add the remaining 1 tablespoon butter and 1 tablespoon of the reserved dredging mixture (discard the remainder). Cook, stirring, until the flour is no longer visible, about 30 seconds. Add the celery-bell pepper mixture, the tomatoes, horseradish, basil, sugar, salt and cayenne, and bring to a boil. Reduce the heat to medium and simmer uncovered, stirring frequently, for 5 minutes.

7 Return the sauce to a boil over medium-high heat. Add the turkey cutlets (and any juices that have accumulated on the plate) to the skillet and cook until the turkey is heated through, about 2 minutes.

Step 7

Values are approximate per serving: Calories: 305 Protein: 30 gm Fat: 15 gm
Carbohydrates: 13 gm Cholesterol: 86 mg Sodium: 550 mg

Chicken-Noodle Soup with Spinach

▼

Homemade chicken soup used to be an all-day project, requiring a stewing hen, soup greens, hours of simmering and a complicated routine of skimming, straining and clarifying. That homemade taste is here without the work, created by cooking chicken thighs in ready-made broth. Noodles, carrots, fresh spinach and corn add old-fashioned richness and depth of flavor.

Working time: 15 minutes
Total time: 30 minutes

Chicken-Noodle Soup
with Spinach

4 Servings

3 cups chicken broth
2 cups water
1 teaspoon thyme
¼ teaspoon pepper
4 large chicken thighs (about
  1¼ pounds total)

2 medium carrots
2 cups packed fresh spinach leaves
  or ½ cup frozen chopped
  spinach, thawed
1 cup egg noodles
1 cup frozen corn

Step 2

1 In a large covered saucepan, bring the chicken broth, water, thyme and pepper to a boil over high heat. Add the chicken thighs and return the liquid to a boil. Reduce the heat to medium-low, cover and simmer for 10 minutes.

2 Meanwhile, cut the carrots into ¼-inch-thick slices. If using fresh spinach, tear the leaves into bite-size pieces.

3 Remove the chicken thighs to a plate. Return the broth to a boil over medium-high heat. Add the carrots and noodles and cook until the noodles are al dente, 4 to 6 minutes, or according to package directions.

4 Meanwhile, skin the chicken thighs, remove the meat from the bone and cut the meat into bite-size pieces (it will still be slightly pink).

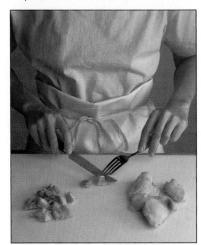

Step 4

5 Return the chicken to the soup. Add the spinach and corn, and cook at a simmer until the chicken is cooked through, about 3 minutes.

TIME-SAVERS

■ ***Do-ahead:*** *The soup can be made ahead and reheated.*

Values are approximate per serving: Calories: 213 Protein: 22 gm Fat: 5 gm
Carbohydrates: 21 gm Cholesterol: 76 mg Sodium: 853 mg

Step 5

Almond Pesto Chicken
with Tomato-Basil Relish

Pesto is as delectable on broiled chicken as it is tossed with pasta. This classic herb sauce is more commonly made with pine nuts or walnuts, but almonds add a deliciously different note. The tomato relish that accompanies this dish is like a light, fresh salsa, fragrant with basil to echo the flavor of the pesto. If you prefer, use chicken breasts only, rather than chicken parts. Serve this entrée straight from the broiler or at room temperature.

Working time: 15 minutes
Total time: 30 minutes

Almond Pesto Chicken with Tomato-Basil Relish

4 Servings

3 cloves garlic
¼ cup blanched almonds
1 cup (packed) fresh basil leaves
plus 2 tablespoons chopped basil
¼ cup plus 2 tablespoons olive or
other vegetable oil
¼ cup grated Parmesan cheese

½ teaspoon salt
⅜ teaspoon pepper
2½ pounds chicken parts
1 pound plum tomatoes
3 tablespoons red wine vinegar or
cider vinegar

1 Preheat the broiler. Line a broiler pan with foil.

2 In a food processor, finely chop the garlic, almonds and 1 cup basil leaves. Add ¼ cup of the olive oil, the Parmesan, salt and ¼ teaspoon of the pepper. Process to a purée.

Step 2

3 Place the chicken on the broiler pan skin-side down. Spoon half of the almond pesto over the chicken and broil 4 inches from the heat for 10 minutes. Turn the chicken over, spread with the remaining almond pesto and broil until the chicken is golden and cooked through, about 10 minutes.

4 Meanwhile, coarsely chop the plum tomatoes. Place them in a small bowl and add the vinegar, the remaining 2 tablespoons olive oil, 2 tablespoons chopped basil and ⅛ teaspoon pepper, and stir to blend.

5 Serve the chicken with the tomato-basil relish on the side.

Step 3

TIME-SAVERS

■ **Do-ahead:** *The almond pesto (Step 2) and tomato-basil relish (Step 4) can both be made ahead.*

Values are approximate per serving: Calories: 593 Protein: 40 gm Fat: 44 gm
Carbohydrates: 11 gm Cholesterol: 114 mg Sodium: 481 mg

Step 4

Thai Turkey, Shrimp and Fruit Salad

▼

The flavors of Thai cuisine—lime, hot pepper and peanuts—combine beautifully with turkey, shrimp and fruit in this refreshing main-dish salad. If you are making the salad in advance and want to use fresh pineapple, however, do not add it until just before serving; otherwise the enzymes in the fresh fruit will break down the fibers in the turkey and shrimp within an hour or so, making them unpleasantly mushy.

Working time: 15 minutes
Total time: 15 minutes

Thai Turkey, Shrimp and Fruit Salad

4 Servings

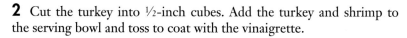

1 small clove garlic
¼ cup fresh mint leaves or
   1 teaspoon dried
⅓ cup lime juice (about 2 limes)
¼ cup Oriental sesame oil
3 tablespoons honey
2 teaspoons grated lime zest (about
   2 limes; optional)
¼ teaspoon red pepper flakes

Pinch of salt
½ pound cooked turkey, unsliced
½ pound cooked baby shrimp
1 navel orange
2 cups pineapple chunks, fresh or
   canned
2 cups seedless red grapes
½ cup unsalted peanuts (optional)

Step 2

1 In a food processor, coarsely chop the garlic. Add the mint and finely chop. Add the lime juice, sesame oil, honey, lime zest (if using), red pepper flakes and salt. Pulse to blend. Transfer the vinaigrette to a large serving bowl.

2 Cut the turkey into ½-inch cubes. Add the turkey and shrimp to the serving bowl and toss to coat with the vinaigrette.

3 Peel the orange, removing all of the bitter white pith. Halve the orange lengthwise and then cut it crosswise into ¼-inch half-rounds.

4 Add the orange, pineapple and grapes to the serving bowl and toss to coat with the vinaigrette.

5 Serve the salad with the peanuts sprinkled on top, if desired.

Step 2

TIME-SAVERS

■ **Do-ahead:** *The vinaigrette (Step 1) can be prepared in advance, the individual ingredients can be cut up ahead of time, or the whole salad can be made ahead.*

Step 4

Values are approximate per serving: Calories: 411   Protein: 30 gm   Fat: 17 gm
Carbohydrates: 37 gm   Cholesterol: 154 mg   Sodium: 205 mg

Chicken and Tiny Star Pasta Stew

▼

The miniature star pasta used here is sometimes labeled "stelline" or "pastina." You could also use alphabets, or orzo (pasta the size and shape of rice grains). In a pinch, break thin spaghetti into 1-inch lengths. If you have some leftover cooked chicken, use it instead of the raw chicken breast; add it at the last minute and cook just until heated through.

Working time: 20 minutes
Total time: 30 minutes

90

Chicken and Tiny Star Pasta Stew

4 Servings

2 large carrots	**3 cups chicken broth**
¼ pound mushrooms	**¾ teaspoon thyme**
1 small bunch scallions (about 6)	**¼ teaspoon pepper**
1 pound skinless, boneless chicken breasts	**½ cup tiny pasta stars, or other small pasta shapes**
2 tablespoons butter	**10 cherry tomatoes**
3 tablespoons flour	

1 Cut the carrots into very thin slices. Cut the mushrooms into thin slices. Coarsely chop the scallions. Cut the chicken into bite-size pieces; set aside.

2 In a large saucepan, melt the butter over medium heat. Stir in the flour and cook, stirring, until the flour has completely absorbed the butter, about 1 minute.

Step 1

3 Increase the heat to medium-high, slowly add a small amount of the chicken broth and stir to combine with the butter and flour. Then add the rest of the chicken broth, the thyme and pepper, and bring to a boil, stirring until slightly thickened.

4 Add the pasta and carrots and cook, uncovered, for 3 minutes.

5 Add the mushrooms, chicken and whole tomatoes. Return the mixture to a boil over medium-high heat, breaking up the tomatoes with a spoon. Reduce the heat to medium-low, cover and simmer until the chicken is cooked through, about 5 minutes.

6 Stir in the scallions and serve hot.

Step 2

TIME-SAVERS

■ ***Do-ahead:*** *The vegetables and chicken can be cut up ahead. The whole stew can be made ahead and reheated gently on the stovetop or in the microwave.*

Values are approximate per serving: Calories: 320 Protein: 32 gm Fat: 8 gm
Carbohydrates: 28 gm Cholesterol: 81 mg Sodium: 649 mg

Step 5

Turkey Scallops with Lemon Slices

▼

Turkey scallops are tremendously versatile; almost any recipe that calls for veal cutlets or chicken breasts can be adapted for this low-fat cut of poultry. Here, the floured scallops are pan-cooked in butter, then the pan juices are transformed into a lemony butter sauce. Bright green beans or yellow wax beans would make a colorful side vegetable, and the sauce can be poured over them as well.

Working time: 25 minutes
Total time: 25 minutes

Turkey Scallops with Lemon Slices

4 Servings

2 lemons
3 tablespoons flour
2 cloves garlic, minced or crushed
  through a press
¼ cup chopped parsley (optional)
½ teaspoon salt

¼ teaspoon pepper
8 small turkey scallops (about
  1½ pounds)
4 tablespoons butter
2 tablespoons olive or other
  vegetable oil

1 Cut one lemon into very thin slices (use whichever lemon has thinner skin). Juice the remaining lemon.

2 In a shallow bowl, combine the flour, garlic, parsley (if using), salt and pepper. Dredge the turkey in the seasoned flour, shaking off any excess.

3 In a large skillet, melt 1 tablespoon of the butter in 1 tablespoon of the oil over medium-high heat until hot but not smoking. Add as many turkey scallops as will fit and cook until golden brown all over, about 3 minutes per side. Keep the turkey warm in a low oven while you cook the remaining turkey in another 1 tablespoon butter in the remaining 1 tablespoon oil.

4 When all of the turkey has been cooked and placed in the oven, add the remaining 2 tablespoons butter and the lemon juice to the skillet. Increase the heat to high and cook, stirring, for 1 minute.

5 Add the lemon slices and cook for about 30 seconds. Arrange the lemon slices over the turkey and pour the lemon sauce on top.

Step 2

Step 3

Step 5

Values are approximate per serving: Calories: 379   Protein: 41 gm   Fat: 21 gm
Carbohydrates: 7 gm   Cholesterol: 137 mg   Sodium: 417 mg

Spicy Chicken-Peanut Stir-Fry

Peanuts and celery add a wonderful crunchiness to this Chinese dish. The celery
and scallions are cut on the diagonal, in traditional Chinese fashion; it's easy to do and
adds an authentic touch. Since scallions play an important role here, choose
fresh, firm ones with crisp greens. Use the whole scallions, white and green, cutting
off only any wilted portions of the green tops.

Working time: 25 minutes
Total time: 25 minutes

Spicy Chicken-Peanut Stir-Fry

4 Servings

4 skinless, boneless chicken breast
   halves (about 1¼ pounds total)
2 tablespoons reduced-sodium or
   regular soy sauce
2 teaspoons Oriental sesame oil
1 tablespoon cornstarch
2 stalks celery
1 bunch scallions (6 to 8)
1 large yellow or green bell pepper
3 quarter-size slices (¼ inch thick)
   fresh ginger, unpeeled

⅔ cup chicken broth
2 drops hot pepper sauce
2 tablespoons olive or other
   vegetable oil
3 cloves garlic, minced or crushed
   through a press
½ cup unsalted peanuts
¼ teaspoon black pepper
¼ cup chopped cilantro (optional)

Step 1

1 Cut the chicken into bite-size pieces. Place the chicken in a bowl and add 1 tablespoon of the soy sauce, the sesame oil and 1½ teaspoons of the cornstarch. Toss to thoroughly coat the chicken.

2 Cut the celery on the diagonal into ½-inch pieces. Cut the scallions on the diagonal into 2-inch lengths. Cut the bell pepper into bite-size pieces. Cut the ginger into slivers.

3 In a small bowl, combine the broth and hot pepper sauce with the remaining 1 tablespoon soy sauce and 1½ teaspoons cornstarch.

4 In a large skillet or wok, warm 1 tablespoon of the olive oil over medium-high heat until hot but not smoking. Add the chicken and its marinade and stir-fry until the chicken is opaque but still slightly pink in the center, about 3 minutes. Transfer the chicken to a plate.

Step 2

5 Add the remaining 1 tablespoon olive oil to the skillet. Add the celery, scallions, bell pepper, ginger and garlic, and stir-fry until the scallions begin to wilt, about 3 minutes.

6 Return the chicken to the skillet and add the peanuts and black pepper. Stir the broth mixture to reblend the cornstarch, add it to the skillet and bring the liquid to a boil. Cook, stirring constantly, until the vegetables are crisp-tender and the chicken is cooked through, about 3 minutes longer. Stir in the cilantro (if using).

TIME-SAVERS

■ *Do-ahead: The chicken can be cut up and combined with its marinade (Step 1) ahead. The vegetables and ginger (Step 2) and seasoned broth (Step 3) can be prepared ahead.*

Values are approximate per serving: Calories: 375 Protein: 39 gm Fat: 20 gm
Carbohydrates: 10 gm Cholesterol: 82 mg Sodium: 579 mg

Step 6

Sautéed Chicken Strips Véronique

▼

*In this variation on the French fish dish, sole Véronique, chicken is cut into strips
—to speed the cooking time—and sautéed with green grapes. The pan juices are then
combined with heavy cream to make a flavorful sauce. The dish calls for
a small amount of white wine, but if you do not already have an open bottle of
wine on hand, just add a bit more chicken broth.*

Working time: 20 minutes
Total time: 20 minutes

Sautéed Chicken Strips Véronique

4 Servings

1½ pounds skinless, boneless chicken breasts
2 tablespoons flour
½ teaspoon salt
¼ teaspoon pepper
2 tablespoons butter
2 tablespoons olive or other vegetable oil

2 cups seedless green grapes
½ cup chicken broth
½ cup heavy cream
2 tablespoons dry white wine (optional)
2 tablespoons chopped parsley (optional)

1 Cut the chicken breasts crosswise into ½-inch-wide strips.

2 In a small bowl, combine the flour, salt and pepper. Toss the chicken strips in the seasoned flour to coat lightly. Set the chicken aside.

3 In a large skillet, melt the butter in the oil over medium-high heat until hot but not smoking. Add the chicken pieces and stir-fry until the chicken just begins to brown, 3 to 4 minutes.

4 Add the grapes, chicken broth, cream and white wine (if using). Let the mixture come to a boil, then reduce the heat to medium-low, cover and simmer, stirring occasionally, until the chicken is cooked through and the grapes are slightly softened, 3 to 4 minutes.

5 Serve the chicken hot, sprinkled with parsley if desired.

TIME-SAVERS

■ **Do-ahead:** *The chicken can be cut up and the grapes washed, stemmed and measured out ahead of time.*

Values are approximate per serving: Calories: 476 Protein: 41 gm Fat: 26 gm
Carbohydrates: 18 gm Cholesterol: 155 mg Sodium: 581 mg

Step 1

Step 2

Step 4

Turkey Cutlets Parmesan with Fresh Tomato Sauce

Adaptable turkey cutlets lend themselves well to this variation on eggplant Parmesan. The cutlets are breaded and sautéed, then cooked briefly with a chunky fresh tomato sauce and topped with a layer of Parmesan and mozzarella. As a side dish, a toss of fresh or roasted peppers and artichokes complements the Italian flavors of the sauce and cheese. For an even more substantial meal, serve the cutlets with spaghetti or linguine.

Working time: 15 minutes
Total time: 25 minutes

Turkey Cutlets Parmesan with Fresh Tomato Sauce

4 Servings

1 pound plum tomatoes	**4 turkey cutlets (about ¾ pound**
1 medium onion	**total)**
¼ cup dry unseasoned	**2 tablespoons olive or other**
breadcrumbs	**vegetable oil**
½ cup grated Parmesan cheese	**2 cloves garlic, minced or crushed**
1¼ teaspoons basil	**through a press**
⅜ teaspoon pepper	**½ cup tomato sauce**
½ teaspoon salt	**½ cup grated part-skim**
1 egg	**mozzarella cheese**

1 Coarsely chop the tomatoes and the onion.

2 In a shallow bowl, combine the breadcrumbs, ¼ cup of the Parmesan, ¼ teaspoon of the basil, ⅛ teaspoon of the pepper and the salt. In another shallow bowl, beat the egg. Dip the turkey cutlets in the beaten egg, then dredge them in the breadcrumb mixture.

Step 3

3 In a large skillet, warm 1 tablespoon of the oil over medium-high heat until hot but not smoking. Add the cutlets and cook until browned all over, about 3 minutes per side. Remove the turkey to a plate and cover loosely to keep warm.

4 Add the remaining 1 tablespoon oil to the skillet. Add the onion and garlic and cook, stirring, for 3 minutes.

5 Add the chopped tomatoes, tomato sauce, the remaining 1 teaspoon basil and ¼ teaspoon pepper. Bring the sauce to a boil over medium heat.

6 Return the turkey to the skillet and sprinkle with the mozzarella and the remaining ¼ cup Parmesan. Reduce the heat to medium-low, cover and simmer until the cheese is melted, about 3 minutes.

Step 5

TIME-SAVERS

■ ***Do-ahead:*** *The vegetables can be cut up and the dredging mixture (Step 2) made ahead.*

Values are approximate per serving: Calories: 317   Protein: 31 gm   Fat: 18 gm
Carbohydrates: 15 gm   Cholesterol: 105 mg   Sodium: 834 mg

Step 6

Hot-and-Sour
Chicken Soup

▼

Hot-and-sour soup originated in the cold northern provinces of China; today, you'll find it on the menu at your local Chinese restaurant, where it is usually made with pork and exotic dried mushrooms. Here, however, chicken and fresh white mushrooms lighten the flavor a bit, while cornstarch and an egg—traditional ingredients—keep the soup deliciously thick. Serve additional hot pepper sauce and vinegar on the side.

Working time: 20 minutes
Total time: 25 minutes

Hot-and-Sour Chicken Soup

4 Servings

3 cups chicken broth
½ cup water
¼ pound small mushrooms
½ cup canned sliced bamboo shoots
3 quarter-size slices (¼ inch thick) fresh ginger, unpeeled
2 cloves garlic, minced or crushed through a press
2 teaspoons reduced-sodium soy sauce

¼ teaspoon hot pepper flakes
1 pound skinless, boneless chicken breast
1 tablespoon Oriental sesame oil
2 scallions
¼ cup cilantro sprigs (optional)
3 tablespoons red wine vinegar or cider vinegar
2 tablespoons cornstarch
1 egg

Step 1

1 In a medium covered saucepan, bring the chicken broth, water, mushrooms, bamboo shoots, ginger, garlic, soy sauce and hot pepper flakes to a boil over medium-high heat. Reduce the heat to low, cover and simmer while you prepare the remaining ingredients.

2 Cut the chicken across the grain into ¼-inch-thick slices. Place the chicken slices in a bowl and toss them with the sesame oil.

3 Finely chop the scallions and the cilantro (if using). In a small bowl, blend the vinegar and cornstarch together. In another small bowl, lightly beat the egg.

Step 2

4 Increase the heat under the broth to medium-high and return it to a boil. Add the chicken slices to the soup. Stirring constantly, slowly pour in the beaten egg. Stir in the vinegar mixture. Cook, stirring occasionally, until the chicken is cooked through and the soup has thickened slightly, about 3 minutes.

5 Stir in the scallions and serve sprinkled with cilantro (if using). If desired, remove the ginger slices before serving.

TIME-SAVERS

■ **Do-ahead:** *All of the individual ingredients can be prepared ahead. The soup can be made through Step 3; bring the soup back to a boil before proceeding.*

Step 4

Values are approximate per serving: Calories: 228 Protein: 31 gm Fat: 7 gm
Carbohydrates: 8 gm Cholesterol: 119 mg Sodium: 933 mg

Chicken Breasts in Tarragon Cream

▼

The tarragon cream sauce that coats these sautéed chicken breasts is reminiscent of a béarnaise, the classic French sauce that is a fragile fusion of egg yolks, butter, vinegar, shallots, and tarragon. Like other egg-based sauces, béarnaise is delicate and must be carefully tended to keep it from curdling. You'll find this recipe much less trouble: The tarragon-scented sauce contains no eggs, and is mixed right in the skillet.

Working time: 15 minutes
Total time: 25 minutes

Chicken Breasts in Tarragon Cream

4 Servings

5 medium shallots or 1 medium onion
3 cloves garlic
3 tablespoons cornstarch
½ teaspoon salt
½ teaspoon pepper
4 skinless, boneless chicken breast halves (about 1¼ pounds total)

1 tablespoon butter
2 tablespoons olive or other vegetable oil
⅔ cup chicken broth
2 teaspoons Dijon mustard
1½ teaspoons tarragon
⅓ cup heavy cream

1 In a food processor, coarsely chop the shallots (or onion) and garlic.

2 In a plastic or paper bag, combine the cornstarch, salt and ¼ teaspoon of the pepper, and shake to mix. Add the chicken and shake to coat lightly. Remove the chicken and reserve the excess seasoned cornstarch.

Step 2

3 In a large skillet, warm the butter in 1 tablespoon of the oil over medium-high heat until the butter is melted. Add the chicken and brown all over, 3 to 4 minutes per side. Remove the chicken to a plate and cover loosely to keep warm.

4 Add the remaining 1 tablespoon oil to the skillet. Add the shallot-garlic mixture to the skillet and cook, stirring, until light golden, 1 to 2 minutes.

5 Return the chicken (and any juices that have accumulated on the plate) to the skillet. Add the chicken broth, mustard, tarragon and the remaining ¼ teaspoon pepper. Bring the mixture to a boil over medium-high heat.

Step 3

6 In a small bowl, blend the cream and the reserved dredging mixture.

7 Stir the cream-cornstarch mixture into the skillet. Bring to a boil, stirring constantly. Reduce the heat to low, cover and simmer until the chicken is cooked through and the sauce is thickened, about 3 minutes.

Values are approximate per serving: Calories: 353 Protein: 34 gm Fat: 19 gm
Carbohydrates: 10 gm Cholesterol: 117 mg Sodium: 645 mg

Step 7

Turkey Taco Salad

▼

*This light, Mexican-inspired salad offers a variety of tastes and textures.
For a lower-calorie version, do not combine the sour cream and salsa when making the
dressing. Instead, serve the salad with separate dollops of salsa and sour
cream, as shown above, and cut the amount of sour cream back to only ¼ cup, allowing
1 tablespoon per serving. Or, use plain yogurt in place of the sour cream.*

Working time: 20 minutes
Total time: 20 minutes

Turkey Taco Salad

4 Servings

⅔ cup mild red salsa	1 can (16 ounces) corn kernels
½ cup sour cream	2 cups cubed (½ inch) cooked
1 tablespoon cumin	turkey (about ½ pound)
¾ teaspoon salt	3 stalks celery
½ teaspoon pepper	8 leaves lettuce
1 can (20 ounces) kidney beans	2 cups unsalted tortilla chips

1 Make the dressing: In a small serving bowl, stir together the salsa, sour cream, cumin, salt and pepper.

2 Drain the kidney beans in a strainer or colander and rinse them under cold running water. Add the corn to the beans and set them aside to drain well.

Step 1

3 Cube the turkey. Cut the celery into ½-inch dice.

4 In a large bowl, combine the beans, corn, turkey and celery, and toss to combine.

5 Shred the lettuce and divide it among 4 salad plates. Spoon the turkey mixture on top of the lettuce. Garnish each serving with tortilla chips, whole or crumbled, and serve with the dressing on the side.

TIME-SAVERS

■ *Do-ahead: The dressing can be made ahead. The salad ingredients can be tossed together ahead of time, although the lettuce should be shredded just before serving. The tortilla chips should not be added until the last moment or they will get soggy.*

Step 2

Values are approximate per serving: Calories: 454   Protein: 25 gm   Fat: 17 gm
Carbohydrates: 53 gm   Cholesterol: 56 mg   Sodium: 939 mg

Step 3

Glazed Chicken Kebabs with Pineapple and Peppers

▼

If you do not have metal skewers, you can make these kebabs on wooden skewers, which are widely available in supermarkets. Just be sure to soak the wooden skewers in cold water for at least 30 minutes before putting them on the grill or under the broiler; this will keep them from burning. Serve the kebabs on a bed of steamed white rice.

Working time: 25 minutes
Total time: 25 minutes

Glazed Chicken Kebabs
with Pineapple and Peppers

4 Servings

1 can (20 ounces) juice-packed pineapple chunks
2 tablespoons cider vinegar
2 tablespoons brown sugar
1 tablespoon cornstarch

½ teaspoon ground ginger
½ teaspoon salt
2 pounds skinless, boneless chicken breasts
2 medium green bell peppers

1 Drain the pineapple, reserving 1 cup of the juice.

2 Make the basting sauce: In a small saucepan, combine the reserved pineapple juice, the vinegar, sugar, cornstarch, ginger and salt and stir to blend. Cook the mixture over medium heat, stirring constantly, until it thickens, about 2 minutes. Remove the pan from the heat and set aside.

Step 3

3 Cut the chicken into 1-inch chunks. Cut the bell peppers into 1-inch squares.

4 Preheat the broiler or start the charcoal. If broiling, line a baking sheet with foil.

5 Dividing the ingredients evenly, thread the chicken cubes, bell pepper squares and pineapple chunks alternately on the skewers.

6 Brush the kebabs with the basting sauce. If broiling, place the kebabs on the baking sheet before brushing them.

Step 5

7 Broil or grill the kebabs 4 inches from the heat for 2 to 3 minutes, or until the chicken begins to brown.

8 Turn the kebabs, brush them with basting sauce and cook them for another 2 to 3 minutes, or until the chicken is opaque.

TIME-SAVERS

■ **Do-ahead:** *The basting sauce can be made ahead. Reheat it briefly to make it easier to brush on the kebabs. The chicken and bell peppers can also be cut up ahead.*

Values are approximate per serving: Calories: 379 Protein: 53 gm Fat: 3 gm
Carbohydrates: 33 gm Cholesterol: 132 mg Sodium: 426 mg

Step 6

Indian-Style Tangy Turkey

▼

The ingredients list may look lengthy for this simple turkey-and-vegetable entrée, but every good Indian cook knows it is a custom-blended spice mixture that gives a dish its unique character. Heating the spices in butter or oil for a moment is another authentic Indian touch: It brings out the essential oils in the seasonings, blends them and ensures that the finished dish will have full, rounded flavors.

Working time: 25 minutes
Total time: 25 minutes

Indian-Style Tangy Turkey

4 Servings

2 cups water
1 cinnamon stick or ¼ teaspoon ground cinnamon
1 cup raw rice
1 medium onion
2 tablespoons butter
1 tablespoon olive or other vegetable oil
3 cloves garlic, minced or crushed through a press
2 teaspoons cumin
1 teaspoon ground ginger
¼ teaspoon nutmeg

Pinch of cayenne pepper
2 tablespoons flour
1 cup canned stewed tomatoes, with their juice
½ cup chicken broth
¼ teaspoon salt
¼ teaspoon black pepper
Pinch of sugar
1 pound turkey scallops
¼ cup sour cream
¼ cup yogurt
1 package (10 ounces) frozen peas
¼ cup chopped cilantro (optional)

Step 4

1 In a medium saucepan, bring the water and cinnamon to a boil over medium-high heat. Add the rice, reduce the heat to medium-low, cover and simmer until the rice is tender and all the liquid is absorbed, about 20 minutes. Discard the cinnamon stick.

2 Meanwhile, cut the onion into thin slices. In a medium skillet, warm 1 tablespoon of the butter in the oil over medium-high heat until the butter is melted. Add the onion and garlic and cook until the mixture is light golden, 3 to 5 minutes.

3 Add the remaining 1 tablespoon butter, the cumin, ginger, nutmeg and cayenne, and cook, stirring, until the spices are fragrant, about 30 seconds. Blend in the flour and cook, stirring, for 30 seconds.

Step 5

4 Add the stewed tomatoes and their juice, the chicken broth, salt, black pepper and sugar. Bring the mixture to a boil, stirring constantly, until the sauce has thickened slightly, about 3 minutes. Reduce the heat to low, cover and simmer while you prepare the turkey.

5 Cut the turkey across the grain into ½-inch-wide strips. In a small serving bowl, blend the sour cream and yogurt.

6 Uncover the sauce and bring it to a boil over medium-high heat. Add the turkey and peas, and cook, stirring frequently, until the turkey is just cooked through, about 5 minutes.

7 Serve the rice topped with the turkey and sauce and sprinkled with the cilantro if desired. Pass the bowl of sour cream-yogurt on the side.

Values are approximate per serving: Calories: 525 Protein: 37 gm Fat: 15 gm
Carbohydrates: 59 gm Cholesterol: 93 mg Sodium: 657 mg

Step 6

Grilled Orange-Cumin Chicken Thighs

▼

If you're making this meal on a weekend, place the chicken in the marinade in the morning or the night before. Although this recipe calls for cooking the chicken with the skin on, it will also be fine if you cook it skinless, since the marinade will keep the chicken moist and flavorful. Serve the chicken with simple side dishes such as corn on the cob and french fries.

Working time: 10 minutes
Total time: 25 minutes

Grilled Orange-Cumin Chicken Thighs

4 Servings

2 cloves garlic, minced or crushed through a press	**2 tablespoons honey**
¼ cup chopped parsley (optional)	**2 tablespoons tomato paste**
½ cup frozen orange juice concentrate	**1½ teaspoons cumin**
2 tablespoons olive or other vegetable oil	**½ teaspoon salt**
	¼ teaspoon pepper
	8 chicken thighs (about 1¾ pounds total)

1 Preheat the broiler or start the charcoal. If broiling, line a broiler pan with foil.

2 In a large bowl, stir together the garlic, parsley (if using), orange juice, oil, honey, tomato paste, cumin, salt and pepper.

Step 2

3 Add the chicken thighs and toss to coat.

4 Arrange the chicken on the broiler pan or grill. Broil or grill the chicken 4 inches from the heat until browned on all sides and the juices run clear, about 10 minutes per side. If desired, brush the chicken with any extra marinade as it broils.

TIME-SAVERS

■ **Do-ahead:** *The chicken can begin to marinate well ahead of time and the whole dish can be cooked ahead and eaten cold.*

Step 3

Step 4

Values are approximate per serving: Calories: 413 Protein: 27 gm Fat: 23 gm
Carbohydrates: 25 gm Cholesterol: 95 mg Sodium: 427 mg

Curried Turkey Salad

This dish is perfect for using up post-holiday turkey leftovers. Or if there are real turkey-lovers in your family, roast a boneless turkey breast to use in sandwiches and in salads like this one. You can also use cooked turkey from the deli or supermarket: ask for an unsliced ½-inch-thick piece, which will make it easy to cut into cubes.

Working time: 15 minutes
Total time: 15 minutes

Curried Turkey Salad

4 Servings

¼ cup reduced-calorie mayonnaise
¼ cup plain yogurt
1 tablespoon orange marmalade, apricot jam or mango chutney (optional)
2 teaspoons curry powder
⅛ teaspoon salt

⅛ teaspoon pepper
1½ cups cubed cooked turkey (about ½ pound)
1 Granny Smith or other tart green apple
1 cup seedless red grapes
½ cup chopped walnuts or pecans

Step 1

1 Make the dressing: In a medium serving bowl, combine the mayonnaise, yogurt, marmalade (if using), curry powder, salt and pepper.

2 Cut the turkey into ½-inch cubes. Core but do not peel the apple and cut it into ½-inch cubes.

3 Add the turkey, apple, grapes and walnuts to the dressing and stir until well combined.

TIME-SAVERS

■ **Do-ahead:** *The dressing can be made and the turkey cubed ahead of time. You can also assemble the entire salad ahead of time and serve it chilled.*

Step 2

Step 3

Values are approximate per serving: Calories: 287   Protein: 20 gm   Fat: 17 gm
Carbohydrates: 17 gm   Cholesterol: 49 mg   Sodium: 205 mg

Chicken Egg Foo Yong with Chinese Cabbage

▼

These savory patties make a wonderful light entrée. Serve them with steamed rice and a crisp salad, such as the cucumber and radish combination shown here. Egg foo yong can also be served as one of several dishes in a Chinese-style meal; just make the portions smaller. If you cannot find Chinese or Napa cabbage, you can make these with regular cabbage, although the flavor will not be as delicate.

Working time: 25 minutes
Total time: 25 minutes

Chicken Egg Foo Yong
with Chinese Cabbage

4 Servings

2 large leaves Chinese or Napa cabbage
2 medium carrots
1 cup cubed cooked chicken (about 5 ounces)
2 tablespoons Oriental sesame oil, or peanut or olive oil

1 cup bean sprouts (about 3 ounces)
2 eggs
½ teaspoon salt
⅛ teaspoon red pepper flakes
2 scallions, chopped, for garnish (optional)

1 Cut the cabbage leaves crosswise into ¼-inch-wide shreds. Coarsely chop the carrots. Cut the chicken into ½-inch cubes.

2 In a large skillet, warm 1 tablespoon of the oil over medium-high heat. Add the bean sprouts, cabbage and carrots and stir-fry until the vegetables just turn limp, about 5 minutes. Transfer the vegetables to a plate and let cool slightly.

Step 1

3 Meanwhile, in a medium bowl, beat the eggs with the salt and red pepper flakes. Add the chicken and stir-fried vegetables and stir well to distribute the ingredients evenly.

4 Warm the remaining 1 tablespoon oil in the skillet over medium-high heat. Measure out about ⅓ cup of the chicken mixture and place it in the skillet, roughly forming it into a round patty with a spatula. Repeat with the remaining mixture. Fry the patties until they are golden on both sides, about 2½ minutes per side.

Step 3

5 Serve hot, garnished with chopped scallions if desired.

TIME-SAVERS

■ *Microwave tip: If you do not have already cooked chicken, you can cook chicken breast quickly in the microwave. Place about ½ pound of skinless, boneless chicken breast in a shallow microwave-safe dish. Cover loosely and cook at 100% for about 4½ minutes, or until the chicken is cooked all the way through.*

■ *Do-ahead: The vegetables and chicken can be cut up ahead of time.*

Values are approximate per serving: Calories: 192 Protein: 14 gm Fat: 12 gm
Carbohydrates: 6 gm Cholesterol: 169 mg Sodium: 354 mg

Step 4

Caribbean Chicken

Caribbean cooks traditionally use sweet fruits and hot spices to complement the savory flavors of meat or poultry. Here, pineapple sparked with hot pepper sauce adds a tropical note to a simple chicken sauté. Colorful bits of yellow and green peppers and aromatic citrus zests further enhance the Caribbean feeling. For dessert, serve a salad of mango, papaya, banana and fresh coconut. Splash with dark rum if desired.

Working time: 15 minutes
Total time: 30 minutes

Caribbean Chicken

4 Servings

2 tablespoons cornstarch
½ teaspoon black pepper
4 skinless, boneless chicken breast
  halves (about 1¼ pounds total)
2 tablespoons vegetable oil
1 medium onion
3 cloves garlic, minced or crushed
  through a press
1 can (8 ounces) crushed pineapple,
  with its juice

¼ teaspoon sugar
3 to 5 drops hot pepper sauce, to
  taste
1 medium green bell pepper
1 medium yellow or red bell pepper
3 tablespoons chopped cilantro
  (optional)
1 navel orange
1 lime
½ teaspoon salt

Step 1

1 In a shallow bowl, combine the cornstarch and black pepper. Lightly dredge the chicken breasts in the seasoned cornstarch.

2 In a large skillet, warm 1 tablespoon of the oil over medium-high heat until hot but not smoking. Add the chicken and brown all over, about 5 minutes per side. Remove the chicken to a plate and cover loosely to keep warm.

3 Meanwhile, coarsely chop the onion.

4 Add the remaining 1 tablespoon oil to the skillet. Add the onion, garlic, pineapple, sugar and hot pepper sauce. Bring the mixture to a boil over medium-high heat. Reduce the heat to low, cover and simmer while you prepare the remaining ingredients.

5 Coarsely chop the green bell pepper. Sliver the yellow bell pepper. Chop the cilantro (if using). Grate the zest from the orange (reserve the orange for another use). Grate the zest from the lime and then juice the lime.

Step 4

6 Return the pineapple mixture to a boil over medium-high heat. Add the bell peppers, orange zest, lime zest, lime juice and salt. Return the chicken (and any juices that have accumulated on the plate) to the skillet. Heat until the chicken is cooked through, about 3 minutes.

7 Stir in the cilantro and serve hot.

TIME-SAVERS

■ *Do-ahead: The vegetables can be cut up ahead. The orange and lime zests can be grated and the lime juiced in advance.*

Values are approximate per serving: Calories: 305 Protein: 34 gm Fat: 9 gm
Carbohydrates: 22 gm Cholesterol: 82 mg Sodium: 373 mg

Step 5

Broiled Turkey with Savory Fruit Marinade

▼

Mild-tasting turkey pairs well with tart-sweet fruit. Here, a mixture of chopped orange, marmalade, scallions, garlic and parsley serves as a chunky topping for broiled turkey cutlets. Apricot jam could be substituted for the marmalade, and tangerines, grapefruit, peaches, nectarines, or even pineapple could be used instead of oranges. Serve the turkey cutlets with simple steamed vegetables, such as squash.

Working time: 10 minutes
Total time: 20 minutes

118

4 Servings

1 orange
4 scallions
2 cloves garlic, minced or crushed through a press
2 tablespoons chopped parsley (optional)
2 tablespoons orange marmalade or apricot jam

1 tablespoon olive or other vegetable oil
½ teaspoon salt
¼ teaspoon pepper
4 turkey cutlets (about 1 pound total)

1 Preheat the broiler. Line a baking sheet with foil and grease it lightly.

2 Peel the orange and remove all of the bitter white pith. Coarsely chop the orange and place it in a medium bowl. Coarsely chop the scallions and add them to the orange.

Step 2

3 Stir in the garlic, parsley (if using), marmalade (or apricot jam), oil, salt and pepper.

4 Place the turkey cutlets on the prepared baking sheet and coat with half of the orange mixture. Broil 4 inches from the heat until browned, about 4 minutes.

5 Turn the turkey over and coat with the remaining orange mixture. Broil 4 inches from the heat until the turkey is cooked through and the topping is golden, about 5 minutes.

Step 3

TIME-SAVERS

■ ***Do-ahead:*** *The orange mixture (Steps 2 and 3) can be made ahead.*

Values are approximate per serving: Calories: 209 Protein: 27 gm Fat: 5 gm
Carbohydrates: 13 gm Cholesterol: 70 mg Sodium: 352 mg

Step 4

Chicken Thighs
with Lime and Curry

▼

*Lime juice, lime zest and sour cream add a lively tartness to the
curry sauce that flavors this chicken dish. Serve it with your favorite
rice pilaf, or simply dress up plain white or brown rice by adding
some chopped scallions, diced carrots, dried apricots, slivered almonds or a
sprinkling of pine nuts. Offer extra lime wedges with the chicken.*

Working time: 25 minutes
Total time: 30 minutes

Chicken Thighs
with Lime and Curry

4 Servings

8 chicken thighs (about 1¾ pounds total)
2 tablespoons flour
¼ teaspoon pepper
1 tablespoon butter
1 tablespoon olive or other vegetable oil
1 medium red onion
2 cloves garlic, minced or crushed through a press

½ cup chicken broth
1½ teaspoons curry powder
3 drops hot pepper sauce
2 teaspoons grated lime zest (optional)
¼ cup lime juice
¼ cup (packed) cilantro sprigs (optional)
⅓ cup sour cream

Step 1

1 Skin the chicken thighs.

2 In a plastic or paper bag, combine the flour and pepper, and shake to mix. Add the chicken and shake to coat lightly. Remove the chicken and reserve the excess seasoned flour.

3 In a large skillet, warm the butter in the oil over medium-high heat until the butter is melted. Add the chicken and cook until golden all over, about 4 minutes per side.

4 Meanwhile, coarsely chop the onion.

5 Remove the chicken to a plate and cover loosely to keep warm. Add the onion and garlic to the skillet and cook for 1 minute. Add the reserved dredging mixture and stir until the flour is no longer visible.

6 Add the chicken broth, curry powder and hot pepper sauce, and bring the mixture to a boil. Reduce the heat to low, cover and simmer while you prepare the rest of the ingredients.

Step 7

7 If using fresh limes, finely grate the zest from the limes and then juice them. Chop the cilantro (if using).

8 Bring the broth mixture to a boil over medium-high heat. Stir in the lime zest, lime juice, 2 tablespoons of the cilantro and the sour cream. Return the chicken (and any juices that have accumulated on the plate) to the skillet. Return to a boil over medium-high heat and cook until the chicken is cooked through and coated with sauce, 4 to 5 minutes.

9 Serve the chicken sprinkled with the remaining cilantro.

Values are approximate per serving: Calories: 264 Protein: 24 gm Fat: 15 gm
Carbohydrates: 7 gm Cholesterol: 110 mg Sodium: 266 mg

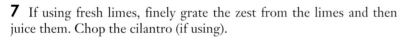

Step 8

Sautéed Turkey Cutlets with Fruit and Walnuts

If your local store doesn't stock cranberries year-round and you don't have a few bags of them tucked away in the freezer, you can substitute raisins (dark or golden) in this recipe. Just remember to omit the sugar since raisins are much sweeter than cranberries. Also note that turkey "cutlets" are often marketed as "breast slices." As an accompaniment to this dish, try steamed Brussels sprouts sautéed with butter and garlic.

Working time: 25 minutes
Total time: 30 minutes

Sautéed Turkey Cutlets with Fruit and Walnuts

4 Servings

¼ cup flour
½ teaspoon salt
¼ teaspoon pepper
8 small turkey cutlets (about 1¼ pounds total)
1 small onion
1 large Granny Smith apple, unpeeled
3 tablespoons butter

3 tablespoons olive or other vegetable oil
1 teaspoon cinnamon
1 teaspoon sugar
½ cup cranberries, fresh or frozen
½ cup apple juice
½ cup chicken broth
½ cup chopped walnuts

1 In a shallow bowl, combine the flour, salt and pepper. Dredge the turkey lightly in the seasoned flour, reserving the excess.

2 Thinly slice the onion. Cut the apple into bite-size pieces.

3 In a large skillet, warm 1 tablespoon of the butter in 1 tablespoon of the oil over medium-high heat until the butter is melted. Add half the turkey and brown all over, 2 to 3 minutes per side. Remove the turkey to a plate and cover loosely to keep warm. Add another 1 tablespoon butter and 1 tablespoon oil. Brown the remaining turkey and add it to the plate with the first batch.

Step 3

4 Add the remaining 1 tablespoon each butter and oil to the skillet. Add the onion and apple, and sauté until the onion begins to brown and the apple is softened, about 4 minutes.

5 Stir in the reserved dredging mixture, cinnamon, sugar and cranberries, and cook, stirring, until the flour is no longer visible, about 30 seconds. Stir in the apple juice and chicken broth, and bring the mixture to a boil, stirring frequently.

Step 4

6 Return the turkey (and any juices that have accumulated on the plate) to the skillet. Reduce the heat to low, cover and simmer until the turkey is just cooked through, 2 to 3 minutes.

7 Meanwhile, if desired, toast the walnuts in an ungreased skillet over medium heat or in an oven or toaster oven at 375°.

8 Serve the turkey topped with some of the sauce and the chopped walnuts.

Values are approximate per serving: Calories: 512 Protein: 37 gm Fat: 31 gm
Carbohydrates: 23 gm Cholesterol: 111 mg Sodium: 583 mg

Step 5

Orange-Apricot Chicken Wings with Carrot Slaw

▼

Chicken wings are a fun finger food, but you can substitute other chicken parts instead if you allow a bit more cooking time. To serve four people, cook eight chicken thighs or drumsticks; the broiling time will be about 20 minutes (10 minutes per side). The fresh carrot-pepper slaw served alongside acts as both a refreshing relish and a salad. If you like, make a double batch and have it with sandwiches the next day.

Working time: 20 minutes
Total time: 30 minutes

Orange-Apricot Chicken Wings
with Carrot Slaw

4 Servings

½ cup plus 1½ teaspoons
   orange juice
¼ cup apricot jam
2 tablespoons honey
1½ tablespoons Dijon mustard
2 teaspoons grated orange zest
   (optional)
2 cloves garlic, minced or crushed
   through a press

⅜ teaspoon black pepper
3 scallions
12 chicken wings
2 large green bell peppers
2 large carrots
2 tablespoons olive or other
   vegetable oil
1½ teaspoons lemon juice
¼ teaspoon salt

Step 3

1 Preheat the broiler. Line a broiler pan with foil.

2 In a large bowl, combine ½ cup of the orange juice, the apricot jam, honey, 1 tablespoon of the mustard, the orange zest (if using), garlic and ¼ teaspoon of the black pepper.

3 Coarsely chop the scallions and stir into the orange-apricot marinade. Add the chicken wings and toss to coat completely.

4 Place the chicken wings, wing tips pointing up, on the prepared broiler pan. Broil 4 inches from the heat for 8 to 10 minutes. Turn the wings over, baste with some more of the marinade and broil until lightly browned, about 8 minutes longer.

5 Meanwhile, in a food processor with a shredding blade, shred the bell peppers and carrots. Place the shredded vegetables in a strainer and press out excess liquid.

Step 4

6 In a medium bowl, combine the olive oil, lemon juice, salt and the remaining 1½ teaspoons orange juice, 1½ teaspoons mustard and ⅛ teaspoon black pepper.

7 Toss the shredded vegetables with the dressing and serve the slaw alongside the broiled chicken wings.

TIME-SAVERS

■ *Microwave tip: To make the jam easier to whisk into the sauce, warm it in a microwave-safe measuring cup or bowl at 100% for 30 seconds to 1 minute. If the honey you have is crystallized or hard to pour, place the jar (without cap) in the microwave for 30 to 45 seconds at 100%.*

■ *Do-ahead: The carrot-pepper slaw can be made well ahead.*

Values are approximate per serving: Calories: 504   Protein: 29 gm   Fat: 27 gm
Carbohydrates: 36 gm   Cholesterol: 86 mg   Sodium: 411 mg

Step 7

Hot Smoked Turkey Sandwich

This delicious take on two lunchtime favorites—a standard turkey sandwich and a gooey grilled cheese—combines the savory flavor of smoked turkey with ripe tomatoes, Swiss cheese and an herbed mayonnaise spread. If you want to make this sandwich in the winter when garden-ripe tomatoes are not available, use one or two large squares of red bell pepper sprinkled with a a few drops of lemon juice or balsamic vinegar.

Working time: 10 minutes
Total time: 15 minutes

Hot Smoked Turkey Sandwich

4 Servings

¼ cup mayonnaise
2 teaspoons Dijon mustard
2 tablespoons chopped parsley
  (optional)
½ teaspoon oregano
½ teaspoon tarragon

⅛ teaspoon pepper
2 medium tomatoes
2 slices rye bread
2 slices pumpernickel bread
½ pound smoked turkey, sliced
¼ pound Swiss cheese, sliced

Step 2

1 Preheat the broiler. Line a broiler pan with foil.

2 In a small bowl, combine the mayonnaise, mustard, parsley (if using), oregano, tarragon and pepper.

3 Thinly slice the tomatoes.

4 Place the bread on the broiler pan. Spread each slice with herbed mayonnaise. Dividing evenly, place the sliced turkey on the bread. Top with tomato slices and then with Swiss cheese.

5 Broil the sandwiches 4 inches from the heat for 3 to 5 minutes, or until the cheese is melted and bubbly.

Step 4

TIME-SAVERS

■ **Do-ahead:** *The herbed mayonnaise can be made ahead.*

Step 4

Values are approximate per serving: Calories: 356 Protein: 22 gm Fat: 22 gm
Carbohydrates: 20 gm Cholesterol: 59 mg Sodium: 943 mg

Turkey-Soba Soup

▼

A Japanese noodle soup is a meal in itself, and there are restaurants in Japan devoted exclusively to these filling entrées. There are several types of Japanese soup noodles, including the soba used here. Soba noodles are made of buckwheat, which gives them a hearty flavor and a firm texture. If you can't find them in your local market, substitute linguine or whole wheat spaghetti, adjusting the cooking time as necessary.

Working time: 20 minutes
Total time: 30 minutes

Turkey-Soba Soup

4 Servings

4 cups chicken broth
2 cups water
3 medium carrots
1 medium red onion
3 quarter-size slices (¼ inch thick)
  fresh ginger, unpeeled
½ pound cooked turkey, sliced
2 teaspoons sesame seeds

½ pound soba noodles
½ pound fresh spinach or 1
  package (10 ounces) frozen leaf
  spinach, thawed
¼ cup chopped cilantro (optional)
2 teaspoons Oriental sesame oil
¼ teaspoon pepper, preferably
  white

Step 2

1 In a large saucepan, bring the chicken broth and water to a boil over medium-high heat.

2 Meanwhile, cut the carrots into matchsticks. Cut the onion into thin wedges. Mince the ginger. Cut the turkey into ½-inch-wide strips.

3 Add the carrots, onion and ginger to the broth. Reduce the heat to low, cover and simmer for 5 minutes.

Step 3

4 Meanwhile, if desired, toast the sesame seeds in a small ungreased skillet over medium heat.

5 Uncover the soup and bring it to a boil over medium-high heat. Add the noodles and cook until al dente, 5 to 8 minutes, or according to package directions. A minute or so before the noodles are done, add the spinach, cilantro (if using), sesame oil and pepper. Continue cooking until the noodles are done and the spinach is wilted.

6 Spoon the broth, noodles and vegetables into soup bowls. Top with the turkey and sesame seeds.

TIME-SAVERS

■ **Do-ahead:** *The recipe can be prepared ahead through Step 4.*

Step 5

Values are approximate per serving: Calories: 385   Protein: 30 gm   Fat: 8 gm
Carbohydrates: 53 gm   Cholesterol: 44 mg   Sodium: 1536 mg

London Broil with Chili Seasonings (page 193)

CHAPTER 3
MEAT

Spicy Fajita Roll-Ups

Although fajitas are Tex-Mex in origin, serving them in lettuce leaves rather than in tortillas adds an Asian accent: The Vietnamese prepare a version of spring rolls with lettuce-leaf wrappers, and the Chinese serve stir-fried foods in lettuce leaf "sandwiches." Here, the traditional fajita filling of grilled beef, onion and bell pepper is enfolded in soft Boston or Bibb lettuce leaves. Serve salsa alongside, if you like.

Working time: 20 minutes
Total time: 30 minutes

Spicy Fajita Roll-Ups

4 Servings

3 tablespoons cider vinegar	**¼ teaspoon red pepper flakes**
1 teaspoon honey	**1 pound flank steak**
1 tablespoon vegetable oil	**1 large onion**
3 cloves garlic, minced or crushed through a press	**1 large red bell pepper**
2 tablespoons chili powder	**8 large Boston or Bibb lettuce leaves**
1 tablespoon cumin	**¼ cup plain yogurt**

1 In a shallow container large enough to hold the steak, combine the vinegar and honey, stirring until well blended. Blend in the oil, garlic, chili powder, cumin and red pepper flakes.

2 Add the flank steak to the marinade and turn to coat completely. Set aside.

Step 2

3 Preheat the broiler. Line a broiler pan with foil.

4 Halve the onion lengthwise, then cut crosswise into thin half-rings. Cut the bell pepper into thin strips.

5 Place the steak on the broiler pan, reserving the marinade. Broil the meat 4 inches from the heat for 7 minutes. Turn the steak over and broil for another 7 minutes, or until medium-rare. Set the steak aside for about 5 minutes before slicing; reserve the pan juices.

6 Meanwhile, scrape the reserved marinade into a medium skillet and warm over medium heat until bubbly. Add the onion and bell pepper, and stir-fry for 1 to 2 minutes. Reduce the heat to low, cover and cook until the vegetables are crisp-tender, about 6 minutes. Remove from the heat; when the steak is done, add the pan juices from the broiler pan to the onion-pepper mixture.

Step 6

7 Thinly slice the steak across the grain. Dividing evenly, place the steak strips and onion-pepper mixture on the lettuce leaves. Top with a dollop of yogurt.

TIME-SAVERS

■ *Do-ahead: The steak can be marinated ahead, or cooked ahead and served at room temperature. The onion-pepper mixture can be prepared ahead and reheated.*

Values are approximate per serving: Calories: 296   Protein: 25 gm   Fat: 17 gm
Carbohydrates: 12 gm   Cholesterol: 60 mg   Sodium: 135 mg

Step 7

Steak with Lemon-Pepper Crust

▼

Lemon adds a new twist to the classic steak au poivre. The steaks are marinated in the fruit's juice, and lemon zest is added to the peppery crust mixture. Although you can use pre-cracked pepper, the dish will be more fragrant if you crack whole peppercorns yourself: Place them under the flat side of a heavy knife or cleaver and smack it sharply with your fist. Serve the steaks with additional lemon wedges if desired.

Working time: 10 minutes
Total time: 30 minutes

4 Servings

2 lemons
2 T-bone steaks (about 2½ pounds total)
4 scallions

4 cloves garlic, minced or crushed through a press
2 tablespoons cracked pepper

Step 2

1 Preheat the broiler or start the charcoal. If broiling, line a broiler pan with foil.

2 Grate the zest from the lemons, then juice them.

3 Place the steaks in a shallow nonaluminum pan and pour the lemon juice over them. Let stand while you prepare the remaining ingredients and while the broiler or grill is preheating. Turn the steaks over after about 5 minutes.

4 Coarsely chop the scallions. In a small bowl, combine the lemon zest, scallions, garlic and cracked pepper.

5 Remove the steaks from the lemon juice. (If broiling, place them on the prepared broiler pan.) Press half of the lemon-pepper mixture onto the top sides of the steaks.

6 Grill or broil the steaks 4 inches from the heat for 7 minutes.

7 Turn the steaks over and press the remaining lemon-pepper mixture onto them. Grill or broil 4 inches from the heat for 7 minutes for rare; 9 minutes for medium-rare; 11 minutes for medium to well-done.

8 Let the steaks stand for 5 minutes before slicing.

Step 3

TIME-SAVERS

■ ***Do-ahead:*** *The lemon-pepper mixture (Step 4) can be prepared ahead. The steaks can be put in the marinade several hours ahead.*

Values are approximate per serving: Calories: 499 Protein: 41 gm Fat: 34 gm
Carbohydrates: 8 gm Cholesterol: 132 mg Sodium: 100 mg

Step 5

Orange Pork Stir-Fry

▼

The mandarin oranges (which are actually tangerines) add just a touch of sweetness to this pork stir-fry. If you'd prefer, you can make this with a fresh orange or tangerine, although it is a bit more work. To make the fresh orange segments easier to eat, remove all of the membrane around them with a sharp paring knife. Tangerine segments can be used unpeeled, but should be seeded.

Working time: 25 minutes
Total time: 25 minutes

Orange Pork Stir-Fry

4 Servings

1 pound boneless pork loin, trimmed of fat

3 tablespoons peanut or other vegetable oil

2 tablespoons reduced-sodium or regular soy sauce

1 tablespoon plus 2 teaspoons cornstarch

1 large green bell pepper

1 bunch scallions (6 to 8)

3 slices (¼ inch thick) unpeeled fresh ginger (optional)

¾ cup beef broth

2 tablespoons ketchup

1 teaspoon grated orange zest (optional)

1 can (11 ounces) mandarin oranges, drained

Step 1

1 Cut the pork with the grain into 2-inch-wide strips. Then cut each strip across the grain into ¼-inch-thick slices.

2 Place the pork slices in a bowl. Add 1 tablespoon each of the oil, soy sauce and cornstarch. Mix gently until the pork is well coated.

3 Cut the bell pepper into 1-inch squares. Cut the scallions into 2-inch lengths. Slice the ginger (if using).

4 In a bowl, stir together the broth, ketchup, orange zest (if using) and the remaining 2 teaspoons cornstarch and 1 tablespoon soy sauce.

5 In a large skillet or wok, warm 1 tablespoon of the oil over medium-high heat. When the oil is very hot but not smoking, add the pork and the marinade and stir-fry until the pork is almost completely browned but still slightly pink in the center, 3 to 4 minutes. Using a slotted spoon, transfer the pork to a plate and set aside.

Step 3

6 Add the remaining 1 tablespoon oil to the skillet. Add the bell pepper, scallions and ginger, and stir-fry until the scallions wilt, 3 to 4 minutes.

7 Return the pork to the skillet. Stir the broth mixture, then stir it into the skillet. Bring the liquid to a boil.

8 Add the oranges and cook, stirring contantly, until the vegetables are crisp-tender and the pork is cooked through, 2 to 3 minutes. Discard the ginger slices before serving.

TIME-SAVERS

■ *Do-ahead: The pork can be cut up and tossed with its marinade (Steps 1 and 2) ahead of time. The scallions and bell pepper can be prepared ahead. The seasoned broth (Step 4) can also be made ahead.*

Values are approximate per serving: Calories: 358   Protein: 26 gm   Fat: 19 gm
Carbohydrates: 22 gm   Cholesterol: 68 mg   Sodium: 623 mg

Step 8

Cheese-Filled Pepper Burgers

▼

Borrowing the idea of steak au poivre, these cheese-filled burgers have cracked black pepper pressed into them before cooking. You can buy pepper already coarsely cracked, or buy whole peppercorns and crack them with the flat side of a large knife or cleaver. These hamburgers can be pan-fried (as in this recipe), broiled or grilled. Serve them on toasted buns with sliced onion, tomato and lettuce.

Working time: 20 minutes
Total time: 20 minutes

4 Servings

¼ pound Monterey jack or pepper
  jack cheese
1 medium onion
1 pound ground round
2 tablespoons Worcestershire or
  steak sauce

1 teaspoon coarsely cracked
  pepper
½ teaspoon salt

Step 2

1 Grate the cheese. Finely chop the onion.

2 In a medium bowl, combine the beef, onion, Worcestershire sauce, ¼ teaspoon of the pepper and the salt and mix gently. Divide the hamburger mixture into 4 equal portions.

3 Flatten each portion of hamburger into a patty and press one-fourth of the cheese into the center.

4 Pull the sides of the hamburger patty up and over the cheese to completely enclose it. Gently reform into a flat patty, making sure the cheese does not poke out.

5 Sprinkle the hamburger patties with the remaining pepper, pressing it gently into the meat.

6 In a large skillet, preferably nonstick, cook the hamburgers over medium-high heat until done: 3 minutes per side for medium-rare, 4 minutes per side for medium, and 5 minutes per side for well-done.

Step 3

TIME-SAVERS

■ *Do-ahead: The hamburger mixture can be made and/or the hamburgers can be stuffed ahead of time.*

Values are approximate per serving: Calories: 338 Protein: 29 gm Fat: 23 gm
Carbohydrates: 3 gm Cholesterol: 94 mg Sodium: 568 mg

Step 4

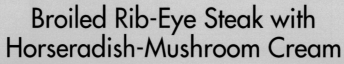

Broiled Rib-Eye Steak with Horseradish-Mushroom Cream

▼

The renowned "roast beef of old England" is often served with a sauce that is a blend of horseradish, heavy cream and mustard. Here, sautéed mushrooms are incorporated into a similar sauce—made with sour cream—and served over generous slices of rib-eye steak. For a simple side dish, brush slices of onion and squash with olive oil and broil them along with the steak.

Working time: 15 minutes
Total time: 25 minutes

Broiled Rib-Eye Steak with Horseradish-Mushroom Cream

4 Servings

2 boneless rib-eye or club steaks
   (about 1½ pounds total)
4 scallions
½ pound mushrooms
2 tablespoons butter
1 tablespoon olive or other
   vegetable oil
2 cloves garlic, minced or crushed
   through a press

½ cup beef broth
1 tablespoon cornstarch
2 tablespoons drained horseradish
1 teaspoon thyme
¼ teaspoon pepper
¼ cup sour cream

Step 5

1 Preheat the broiler. Line a broiler pan with foil.

2 Place the steaks on the prepared broiler pan and broil 4 inches from the heat for 7 minutes. Turn the steaks over and broil for 7 minutes longer for rare; 9 minutes for medium-rare; 11 minutes for medium to well-done. Let the steaks rest for 5 minutes before slicing them.

3 Meanwhile, coarsely chop the scallions. Slice the mushrooms.

4 In a medium skillet, warm the butter in the oil over medium-high heat until the butter is melted. Add the scallions and garlic, and cook until the scallions are limp, about 1 minute.

5 Add the mushrooms and cook, stirring, until the mushrooms start to wilt, about 3 minutes.

Step 6

6 In a small bowl, combine the beef broth and cornstarch. Stir this mixture, the horseradish, thyme and pepper into the skillet. Bring the mixture to a boil over medium heat and cook, stirring, until slightly thickened, 1 to 2 minutes.

7 Stir in the sour cream and remove the horseradish-mushroom cream from the heat.

8 Serve slices of the steak topped with some of the horseradish-mushroom cream.

TIME-SAVERS

■ *Do-ahead: The horseradish-mushroom cream can be made ahead through Step 6; gently reheat and stir in the sour cream off the heat.*

Values are approximate per serving: Calories: 431 Protein: 36 gm Fat: 28 gm
Carbohydrates: 8 gm Cholesterol: 120 mg Sodium: 271 mg

Step 7

Pork Parmesan

▼

Veal Parmesan is an established favorite, and the same treatment works perfectly well with pork. In this recipe, boneless pork cutlets are dipped in egg white, then dredged in breadcrumbs mixed with Parmesan cheese, oregano and pepper. Since the thin pork scallops cook in a matter of minutes, before you sauté them, make a salad—arugula, radicchio, artichoke and bell pepper, for example—and slice a loaf of good Italian bread.

Working time: 10 minutes
Total time: 15 minutes

Pork Parmesan

4 Servings

1 lemon
3 tablespoons fine unseasoned breadcrumbs
3 tablespoons grated Parmesan cheese
1½ teaspoons oregano

½ teaspoon pepper
1 egg white
4 boneless pork cutlets (about ¼ inch thick, 1¼ pounds total)
1 tablespoon butter
2 tablespoons vegetable oil

1 Cut the lemon into wedges and set aside.

2 In a shallow bowl, combine the breadcrumbs, Parmesan, oregano and pepper. In another shallow bowl, beat the egg white until frothy.

3 Dip the pork cutlets into the egg white, just to coat lightly. Then dip the cutlets into the seasoned breadcrumbs.

4 In a large skillet, warm the butter in 1 tablespoon of the oil over medium-high heat until the butter is melted. Add the pork and cook until golden brown and cooked through, about 3 minutes per side. Add the remaining 1 tablespoon oil, if necessary, to prevent sticking.

5 Serve the hot pork with the lemon wedges on the side.

TIME-SAVERS

■ **Do-ahead:** *The dredging mixture (Step 2) can be made ahead.*

Step 2

Step 3

Step 4

Values are approximate per serving: Calories: 326   Protein: 32 gm   Fat: 19 gm
Carbohydrates: 7 gm   Cholesterol: 107 mg   Sodium: 226 mg

Simple Beef Burgundy

The Oriental technique of stir-frying is used here to simplify a traditional French dish. The beef for this version of boeuf bourguignon is cut into strips to reduce the cooking time. Serve the beef burgundy with buttered noodles or rice, steamed green beans and the same red wine used to make the dish. If you would prefer to leave the wine out of this dish, or do not have any on hand, use beef broth in its place.

Working time: 30 minutes
Total time: 30 minutes

Simple Beef Burgundy

4 Servings

1 pound flank steak
½ cup dry red wine
½ pound mushrooms
1 bunch scallions (6 to 8)
4 tablespoons butter
2 cloves garlic, minced or crushed
through a press

2 tablespoons flour
½ teaspoon salt
¼ teaspoon pepper
¼ cup beef broth
1 teaspoon tarragon
¼ cup chopped parsley
(optional)

Step 3

1 Cut the steak with the grain into about 2-inch-wide strips. Then cut each strip across the grain into ¼-inch-thick slices.

2 Place the sliced beef in a medium bowl, add the wine and let marinate at room temperature while you prepare the vegetables.

3 Cut the mushrooms into ¼-inch slices. Cut the scallions into 2-inch lengths.

4 In a large skillet, melt 2 tablespoons of the butter over medium heat until hot but not smoking. Add the garlic, mushrooms and scallions and stir-fry until the mushrooms are limp, about 5 minutes. Scoop the vegetables and pan juices into a bowl and set aside.

Step 4

5 Place the flour, salt and pepper in a plastic or small paper bag.

6 Reserving the marinade, drain the beef in a colander or strainer. Place the drained beef in the bag of seasoned flour and shake to coat.

7 Wipe the skillet dry with paper towels. Add the remaining 2 tablespoons butter and melt over medium-high heat. Add the beef and stir-fry until browned, 3 to 4 minutes.

8 Add the sautéed vegetables and any liquid, the reserved marinade, the broth and tarragon. Bring to a boil and cook, stirring, until the sauce thickens, 1 to 2 minutes.

9 Serve hot, sprinkled with parsley if desired.

TIME-SAVERS

■ ***Do-ahead:*** *The beef can be cut up and mixed with the red wine marinade (Step 2) ahead of time. The mushrooms and scallions can be cut up ahead of time. The mushrooms, scallions and garlic can be sautéed (Step 4) an hour or so before the final cooking of the dish.*

Values are approximate per serving: Calories: 324 Protein: 26 gm Fat: 21 gm
Carbohydrates: 8 gm Cholesterol: 99 mg Sodium: 510 mg

Step 8

Milanese Meatball Heros

Using veal instead of beef or pork and a lemon-garlic mayonnaise
instead of tomato sauce gives this pizza-parlor favorite a whole new twist.
Lightly toasted hero rolls are spread with the seasoned mayonnaise
(which has been lightened with yogurt) and topped with sautéed herbed
meatballs and slices of fresh tomato.

Working time: 30 minutes
Total time: 30 minutes

4 Servings

2 medium tomatoes
⅓ cup (packed) parsley sprigs
1 egg white
2 tablespoons tomato paste
2 tablespoons fine unseasoned
  breadcrumbs
3 cloves garlic, minced or crushed
  through a press
1½ teaspoons oregano
¾ teaspoon salt
½ teaspoon black pepper
¼ teaspoon red pepper flakes

1 pound ground veal
1 tablespoon olive or other
  vegetable oil
4 small hero rolls (about 4½ inches
  long) or 2 long rolls (each about 9
  inches long)
¼ cup mayonnaise
2 tablespoons plain yogurt
½ teaspoon lemon juice
2 teaspoons grated lemon zest
  (optional)

Step 3

1 Preheat the broiler. Thinly slice the tomatoes. Mince the parsley.

2 In a medium bowl, lightly beat the egg white. Beat in 2 tablespoons of the parsley, the tomato paste, breadcrumbs, 2 of the garlic cloves, the oregano, salt, black pepper and red pepper flakes.

3 Add the veal to the egg-white mixture and mix until well blended. Form the mixture into 24 slightly flattened meatballs (about 1 heaping tablespoon each).

4 In a large nonstick skillet, warm the oil over medium-high heat until hot but not smoking. Add the meatballs and cook until well browned on the outside and medium-rare on the inside, about 6 minutes. Remove the meatballs to a plate and cover loosely to keep warm.

Step 4

5 Meanwhile, split the rolls in half horizontally (if using long rolls, cut them in half crosswise first). Place them on a broiler pan and broil 4 inches from the heat until toasted, 30 seconds to 1 minute.

6 In a small bowl, combine the remaining parsley, 1 clove of garlic, the mayonnaise, yogurt, lemon juice and lemon zest (if using).

7 Spread the rolls lightly with the lemon-garlic mayonnaise. Top with the tomato slices. Place 6 meatballs in each sandwich.

TIME-SAVERS

■ **Do-ahead:** *The meatballs can be formed ahead, or cooked ahead and served at room temperature. The lemon-garlic mayonnaise (Step 6) can be made well ahead.*

Values are approximate per serving: Calories: 494 Protein: 30 gm Fat: 24 gm
Carbohydrates: 39 gm Cholesterol: 103 mg Sodium: 1,006 mg

Step 7

Pork Chops Diablo

▼

With no fewer than six piquant ingredients, this fiery dish lives up to the name "diablo." If you wish to temper the spiciness a bit, start by using less hot pepper sauce; to cool the sauce still further, add a little less chili powder. With such a flavorful entrée, keep the side dishes simple: Potatoes or mixed vegetables can share the sauce and onions, and a simple green salad will balance the menu nicely.

Working time: 15 minutes
Total time: 30 minutes

Pork Chops Diablo

4 Servings

1 large onion
⅓ cup flour
2 tablespoons chili powder
¼ teaspoon black pepper
Pinch of cayenne pepper
4 small center-cut pork chops, well trimmed (½ inch thick, about ¾ pound total)

2 teaspoons vegetable oil
1 tablespoon butter
1 can (8 ounces) tomato sauce
⅓ cup beef broth
2 teaspoons Worcestershire sauce
4 to 5 drops hot pepper sauce, to taste
1 teaspoon dry mustard

Step 3

1 Cut the onion into thin wedges.

2 In a plastic or paper bag, combine the flour, chili powder, black pepper and cayenne, and shake to mix. Add the pork chops and shake to coat lightly. Remove the chops and reserve 1 tablespoon of the seasoned flour.

3 In a large skillet, warm the oil over medium-high heat until hot but not smoking. Add the pork chops and cook until browned all over, about 3 minutes per side. Remove the chops to a plate and cover loosely to keep warm.

4 Add the butter and the onion to the skillet and sauté until the onion begins to brown, about 3 minutes.

5 Stir in the reserved 1 tablespoon dredging mixture and cook, stirring, until the flour is no longer visible, about 30 seconds. Add the tomato sauce, beef broth, Worcestershire sauce, hot pepper sauce and mustard.

Step 4

6 Pour any juices that have accumulated under the chops into the skillet and bring the mixture to a boil over medium-high heat, stirring constantly. Add the chops, reduce the heat to low, cover and simmer until the chops are cooked through, about 12 minutes; turn the chops over after 6 minutes.

7 Serve the chops topped with sauce and onions.

TIME-SAVERS

■ *Do-ahead: The onion can be cut up and the dredging mixture (Step 2) prepared ahead.*

Values are approximate per serving: Calories: 253 Protein: 22 gm Fat: 12 gm
Carbohydrates: 15 gm Cholesterol: 61 mg Sodium: 549 mg

Step 6

Veal Scallopini with Sautéed Cherry Tomatoes

▼

Veal scallopini is a classic dinner-party dish. The juicy, mild-flavored meat is a perfect foil for imaginative sauces and side dishes; and although veal scallops are not inexpensive, there is no waste and they cook in minutes, leaving you time to attend to other party details. This recipe is particularly efficient since an attractive vegetable garnish is cooked along with the meat. Round the meal out with rice or pasta.

Working time: 20 minutes
Total time: 25 minutes

Veal Scallopini with Sautéed Cherry Tomatoes

4 Servings

12 cherry tomatoes
¼ pound mushrooms
3 scallions
3 tablespoons flour
¼ teaspoon salt
¼ teaspoon pepper
1 egg

1 pound veal scallopini (about 8
  scallops)
¼ cup olive or other vegetable oil
¾ cup beef broth
1 tablespoon fresh dill or
  1 teaspoon dried

1 Halve the tomatoes. Slice the mushrooms. Coarsely chop the scallions.

2 In a shallow bowl or plate, combine the flour with the salt and pepper. In another bowl, beat the egg. Dip the veal first in the beaten egg and then in the seasoned flour. Reserve the excess flour mixture.

Step 2

3 In a large skillet, warm 2 tablespoons of the oil over medium-high heat until hot but not smoking. Add the veal (in batches if necessary) and cook until golden, about 3 minutes per side. Remove the veal to a plate and cover loosely to keep warm.

4 Add the remaining 2 tablespoons oil to the skillet over medium-high heat. Add the tomatoes, mushrooms and scallions and stir-fry for 2 minutes.

5 Add the reserved flour mixture and stir until the flour is no longer visible. Add the beef broth and bring to a boil, stirring until the sauce has thickened slightly. Reduce the heat to medium-low, cover and simmer until the vegetables are just tender, about 3 minutes.

6 Stir the dill into the vegetables and serve the veal topped with the vegetables and pan juices.

Step 3

TIME-SAVERS

■ *Do-ahead: The vegetables can be cut up ahead.*

Values are approximate per serving: Calories: 301 Protein: 28 gm Fat: 17 gm
Carbohydrates: 8 gm Cholesterol: 142 mg Sodium: 383 mg

Step 4

Oriental Noodle Soup with Carrots, Ham and Zucchini

▼

Although this Oriental noodle soup may look complicated, it is in fact extremely quick and simple to prepare. The seasoned broth is brought to a boil and used to cook the noodles. Then the remaining ingredients (ham, lettuce, zucchini and carrots) are arranged on top of the noodles and broth and cooked for only 2 minutes. The soup can either be brought to the table in the pot or ladled into soup bowls.

Working time: 20 minutes
Total time: 20 minutes

Spicy Oriental Hamburgers with Orange Sauce

4 Servings

4 scallions
1 can (8 ounces) whole or sliced
    water chestnuts, drained
1 pound lean ground beef
4 cloves garlic, minced or crushed
    through a press
1¼ teaspoons grated orange zest
    (optional)
¼ teaspoon red pepper flakes
1 teaspoon vegetable oil

1 teaspoon Oriental sesame oil
¼ cup frozen orange juice
    concentrate, thawed
2 tablespoons reduced-sodium or
    regular soy sauce
1 tablespoon honey
1 tablespoon tomato paste
¼ teaspoon pepper
¼ cup chicken broth
1 teaspoon cornstarch

Step 2

1 In a food processor, coarsely chop the scallions and set aside. In the same work bowl, coarsely chop the water chestnuts.

2 In a medium bowl, combine the beef with half the garlic, half the scallions, all of the water chestnuts, the orange zest (if using) and red pepper flakes. Form the mixture into four equal patties about ⅜ inch thick.

3 In a large skillet, warm the vegetable and sesame oils over medium-high heat until hot but not smoking. Add the hamburgers and cook for about 3 minutes per side for medium-rare; 4 minutes per side for medium; 5 minutes per side for well-done.

Step 3

4 Remove the hamburgers to a plate and cover loosely to keep warm. Reduce the heat under the skillet to medium and add the remaining garlic and scallions, the orange juice concentrate, soy sauce, honey, tomato paste and pepper. Bring to a boil.

5 Meanwhile, in a small bowl or measuring cup, combine the chicken broth and cornstarch. When the mixture in the skillet comes to a boil, stir in the cornstarch mixture and cook, stirring, until slightly thickened, 2 to 3 minutes.

6 Serve the hamburgers topped with some of the sauce.

TIME-SAVERS

■ **Do-ahead:** *The hamburger mixture can be formed into patties ahead of time.*

Step 5

Values are approximate per serving: Calories: 414 Protein: 22 gm Fat: 26 gm
Carbohydrates: 22 gm Cholesterol: 85 mg Sodium: 479 mg

Salisbury Steaks with Savory Sauce

Salisbury steak, often described as a dressed-up hamburger, is truly glorified in this recipe. Here, lean ground beef patties—mixed with vegetables and breadcrumbs to keep them juicy—are broiled, then topped with a thick, flavorful sauce. Serve the steaks with a vegetable side dish, such as buttered lima beans or a baked potato; plain buttered noodles would be good, too.

Working time: 15 minutes
Total time: 25 minutes

4 Servings

¼ **pound mushrooms**
2 stalks celery
1 medium onion
2 cloves garlic
1 pound lean ground beef
⅔ cup fine unseasoned breadcrumbs

½ teaspoon salt
¼ teaspoon pepper
2 tablespoons butter
1 cup beef broth
2 tablespoons tomato paste
4 tablespoons chopped chives (optional)

Step 3

1 Preheat the broiler. Line a broiler pan with foil.

2 In a food processor, coarsely chop the mushrooms, celery, onion and garlic.

3 Remove half of the chopped vegetables to a bowl and combine well with the ground beef, ⅓ cup of the breadcrumbs, the salt and pepper.

4 Form the mixture into patties, a scant ½ inch thick. Place the patties on the broiler pan and broil 4 inches from the heat for 5 minutes. Turn over and broil for 7 minutes longer, or until browned on top.

Step 4

5 Meanwhile, in a medium skillet, melt the butter over medium-high heat until hot but not smoking. Add the reserved chopped vegetables to the skillet and sauté until the onion is slightly softened, about 2 minutes.

6 Stir in the beef broth, tomato paste and remaining ⅓ cup breadcrumbs. Bring the mixture to a boil. Reduce the heat to medium-low, cover and simmer about 5 minutes (or until the beef patties are finished broiling). Just before serving, stir in the chives (if using).

TIME-SAVERS

■ **Do-ahead:** *The patties can be formed ahead of time. The sauce can be made ahead and reheated (add a bit more beef broth if it seems too thick).*

Step 6

Values are approximate per serving: Calories: 380   Protein: 25 gm   Fat: 23 gm
Carbohydrates: 18 gm   Cholesterol: 90 mg   Sodium: 811 mg

Hawaiian Pork Skillet

▼

When pineapple and pork are stir-fried, along with bell pepper, scallions and ginger, a savory Polynesian-style dish is born. Dredging the meat in cornstarch—a traditional Chinese technique—produces a velvety coating on the pork and a lightly thickened sauce for the dish. Unlike flour-based dredging mixtures, the cornstarch coating will make the meat seem gummy before it is cooked, but don't be concerned.

Working time: 25 minutes
Total time: 25 minutes

162

4 Servings

1 pound boneless pork loin
1 can (8 ounces) juice-packed pineapple chunks
3 tablespoons reduced-sodium or regular soy sauce
1 large red bell pepper
4 scallions
4 quarter-size slices (¼ inch thick) fresh ginger, unpeeled

1 tablespoon cornstarch
1 tablespoon vegetable oil
1 tablespoon Oriental sesame oil
2 cloves garlic, minced or crushed through a press
¼ teaspoon black pepper

Step 1

1 Cut the pork loin lengthwise into quarters. Cut each strip of pork crosswise into ¼-inch-thick slices.

2 Drain the canned pineapple, reserving the juice. Place the pineapple juice and soy sauce in a medium bowl. Add the pork slices and toss to coat.

3 Cut the bell pepper into thin slivers. Coarsely chop the scallions. Mince the ginger.

4 Remove the pork from the pineapple-soy mixture, reserving the liquid. Toss the pork with the cornstarch (the pork will be somewhat gummy).

5 In a large skillet, warm the vegetable and sesame oils over medium-high heat until hot but not smoking. Add the ginger and garlic and stir-fry for 1 minute.

6 Add the pork and cook until well browned, about 6 minutes.

Step 1

7 Add the bell pepper, scallions, black pepper and reserved pineapple-soy mixture, and bring to a boil over medium-high heat. Cook, stirring, until the sauce thickens slightly and the bell pepper begins to soften, about 2 minutes.

8 Add the pineapple chunks and cook until they are heated through, 1 to 2 minutes.

TIME-SAVERS

■ **Do-ahead:** *The pork can be cut up and combined with the pineapple-soy marinade ahead. The bell pepper, scallions and garlic can be cut up ahead.*

Values are approximate per serving: Calories: 441   Protein: 23 gm   Fat: 32 gm
Carbohydrates: 16 gm   Cholesterol: 79 mg   Sodium: 517 mg

Step 4

Grilled Beef Salad with Thai Dressing

▼

Thai cooking relies heavily on a condiment called "nam pla," a pungent sauce made from fish or shrimp that's used in much the same way soy sauce is used in Chinese cooking. Here, anchovy paste in the salad dressing suggests the flavor of nam pla, but you can use 2 tablespoons of reduced-sodium soy sauce instead. For extra flavor, toast the sesame seeds in an ungreased skillet over medium heat for 3 to 5 minutes.

Working time: 25 minutes
Total time: 30 minutes

Grilled Beef Salad with Thai Dressing

4 Servings

4 quarter-size slices (¼ inch thick) fresh ginger, unpeeled	**¼ cup lemon juice**
¼ cup plus 2 tablespoons vegetable oil	**3 tablespoons lime juice**
2 tablespoons reduced-sodium soy sauce	**1 teaspoon grated lime zest (optional)**
3 cloves garlic, minced or crushed through a press	**2 drops hot pepper sauce**
2 teaspoons granulated sugar	**1 tablespoon anchovy paste**
¼ teaspoon pepper	**1 tablespoon brown sugar**
1¼ pounds flank steak	**3 plum tomatoes**
¼ cup (packed) fresh mint leaves or 2 teaspoons dried	**1 small cucumber**
	3 scallions
	3 cups shredded iceberg lettuce
	¼ pound bean sprouts
	2 teaspoons sesame seeds

Step 2

1 Preheat the broiler or start the charcoal. If broiling, line a broiler pan with foil.

2 Mince the ginger. In a small bowl, combine half the ginger with 2 tablespoons of the oil, the soy sauce, 2 of the garlic cloves, the granulated sugar and pepper.

3 Brush the steak with half of the ginger basting mixture and grill or broil 4 inches from the heat for 4 minutes. Turn the steak over, brush with the remaining ginger basting mixture and cook another 5 minutes for rare; 6 minutes for medium-rare; 7 minutes for medium. Let the steak stand for 5 minutes before slicing.

4 Meanwhile, in a food processor, mince the fresh mint (if using). Add the lemon and lime juices, lime zest (if using), the hot pepper sauce, anchovy paste, brown sugar, and the remaining minced ginger, garlic clove and ¼ cup oil. Process to blend.

Step 6

5 Cut the tomatoes and cucumber into bite-size cubes. Coarsely chop the scallions. Shred the lettuce. In a large bowl, toss the tomatoes, cucumber, scallions, lettuce and bean sprouts together.

6 Cut the steak with the grain into strips, then cut the strips crosswise into thin slices. Arrange the vegetables on individual dinner plates. Top with steak slices, dressing and sesame seeds.

TIME-SAVERS

■ ***Do-ahead:*** *The basting mixture (Step 2) and dressing (Step 4) can be made and the steak grilled ahead.*

Values are approximate per serving: Calories: 498 Protein: 31 gm Fat: 35 gm
Carbohydrates: 16 gm Cholesterol: 72 mg Sodium: 539 mg

Step 6

Dijon Burgers with Grilled Onions

Your family will never tire of char-broiled burgers if you make subtle changes in the meat mixture each time you grill. These extra-juicy patties are flavored with Dijon mustard, red wine and tarragon, and topped with golden grilled onion slices. To underscore the French connection, hold the ketchup and send the burgers to the table with a crock of Dijon mustard instead.

Working time: 15 minutes
Total time: 25 minutes

Dijon Burgers with Grilled Onions

4 Servings

1 pound lean ground beef
½ cup fine unseasoned breadcrumbs
¼ cup plus 2 tablespoons Dijon mustard
¼ cup dry red wine
1 egg

2 teaspoons tarragon
½ teaspoon pepper
1 large red onion
1 large yellow onion
2 tablespoons olive or other vegetable oil

1 Preheat the broiler or start the charcoal. If broiling, line a broiler pan with foil.

2 In a medium bowl, combine the beef, breadcrumbs, 2 tablespoons of the mustard, 3 tablespoons of the red wine, the egg, 1 teaspoon of the tarragon and ¼ teaspoon of the pepper. Form the meat mixture into 4 patties.

3 Cut the onions crosswise into ½-inch rounds.

4 In a small bowl, combine the remaining ¼ cup mustard, 1 tablespoon red wine, 1 teaspoon tarragon, ¼ teaspoon pepper and the oil, and whisk to blend well.

5 Brush the burgers and onion slices with half of the mustard mixture (if broiling, place them on the broiler pan first) and grill or broil 4 inches from the heat for 5 minutes.

6 Turn the burgers and onions over and brush with the remaining mustard mixture. Grill or broil for 4 minutes longer for medium-rare; 5 minutes for medium; 6 to 7 minutes for well-done.

TIME-SAVERS

■ **Do-ahead:** *The patties can be formed and the mustard mixture (Step 4) made ahead.*

Values are approximate per serving: Calories: 425 Protein: 25 gm Fat: 26 gm
Carbohydrates: 19 gm Cholesterol: 128 mg Sodium: 851 mg

Step 2

Step 3

Step 5

Kielbasa with Apples, Cabbage and Celery

▼

Cabbage with apples is a traditional German dish; cabbage with sausage is likewise an Old Country favorite. Here, the two ideas are combined, and flavored with onions, garlic and celery, to make a thoroughly satisfying dinner. The meaty slices of kielbasa (for which you could substitute beef, pork or turkey sausage) are served atop the savory vegetables. Accompany with dark rye bread and German-style mustard.

Working time: 25 minutes
Total time: 30 minutes

Kielbasa with Apples, Cabbage and Celery

4 Servings

1 pound kielbasa or other garlic sausage
1 medium onion
1 tablespoon plus 1 teaspoon olive or other vegetable oil
3 cloves garlic, minced or crushed through a press
3 cups shredded cabbage (about ¼ pound)

2 medium Granny Smith apples, unpeeled
2 ribs celery
⅓ cup apple juice
⅓ cup chicken broth
1 tablespoon cornstarch
½ teaspoon crumbled sage
½ teaspoon celery seed
¼ teaspoon pepper

1 Bring a large saucepan of water to a boil.

2 Meanwhile, cut the kielbasa on the diagonal into scant ½-inch slices. Add them to the boiling water and cook for 3 minutes. Drain in a colander.

3 Coarsely chop the onion.

4 In a large skillet, warm 1 tablespoon of the oil over medium-high heat until hot but not smoking. Add the onion and garlic and stir-fry until the mixture begins to brown, about 5 minutes.

5 Shred the cabbage. Cut the apple into ¼-inch slices and then into bite-size pieces. Coarsely chop the celery.

6 Add the cabbage, apple and celery to the skillet. Cook, stirring, until the vegetables have softened, about 3 minutes. Transfer the sautéed vegetables to a serving platter and cover loosely to keep warm.

7 Add the remaining 1 teaspoon oil to the skillet. Add the kielbasa and cook until it begins to brown, 3 to 4 minutes.

8 Meanwhile, in a small bowl, combine the apple juice, chicken broth, cornstarch, sage, celery seed and pepper. Add the mixture to the skillet and bring to a boil, stirring, until the sauce has thickened slightly, 2 to 3 minutes.

9 Spoon the hot kielbasa and sauce over the sautéed vegetables.

TIME-SAVERS

■ *Do-ahead: The kielbasa can be parboiled (Step 2) ahead and the onion, cabbage and celery can be cut up in advance.*

Values are approximate per serving: Calories: 474 Protein: 16 gm Fat: 36 gm
Carbohydrates: 22 gm Cholesterol: 76 mg Sodium: 1327 mg

Step 2

Step 5

Step 6

Pork Chops with Lemon-Soy Sauce Glaze

▼

A marinade made with soy sauce, lemon juice, tomato paste and sugar coats these pork chops with a shiny, sweet-and-sour glaze. If you can leave the chops to marinate for a few hours, or overnight, so much the better: they will absorb more of the flavors. Accompany the pork chops with white rice or lightly buttered pasta and steamed vegetables, such as the carrots and shredded Napa cabbage shown here.

Working time: 30 minutes
Total time: 30 minutes

Pork Chops with Lemon-Soy Sauce Glaze

4 Servings

⅓ cup reduced-sodium or regular
  soy sauce
¼ cup lemon juice
¼ cup beef broth
2 tablespoons tomato paste
1 tablespoon brown sugar
2 teaspoons grated lemon zest
  (optional)

1 teaspoon ground ginger
¼ teaspoon pepper
4 lean center-cut pork chops
  (½ inch thick, about 1¼
  pounds total)
1 bunch scallions (6 to 8)
2 tablespoons vegetable oil
¼ cup cornstarch

Step 1

1 In a small bowl, combine the soy sauce, lemon juice, beef broth, tomato paste, brown sugar, lemon zest (if using), ginger and pepper.

2 Place the chops in a shallow container that will hold them in one layer. Pour the lemon-soy sauce over the chops and let them marinate.

3 Coarsely chop the scallions. In a large skillet, warm 1 tablespoon of the oil over medium-high heat until hot but not smoking. Add the scallions and cook, stirring occasionally, until they are just limp, about 3 minutes. Remove the scallions to a plate and set aside.

Step 2

4 Remove the pork chops from the marinade, reserving the marinade. Dredge the pork chops in the cornstarch. Add the remaining 1 tablespoon oil to the skillet and cook the pork chops over medium-high heat until golden, about 3 minutes per side.

5 Add the reserved marinade to the skillet and bring to a boil, turning the chops once. Simmer the pork chops until cooked through, about 8 minutes longer. Stir in the scallions and serve hot.

TIME-SAVERS

■ *Do-ahead: The marinade (Step 1) can be made ahead and the pork chops can be left to marinate for several hours or overnight.*

Step 4

Values are approximate per serving: Calories: 325 Protein: 28 gm Fat: 16 gm
Carbohydrates: 17 gm Cholesterol: 75 mg Sodium: 993 mg

Stovetop Barbecued Burgers

▼

A generous topping of tangy barbecue sauce sparked with orange juice and chili powder brings a taste of summer to these juicy burgers. The recipe calls for the beef patties to be pan-fried, but if you prefer broiled or grilled hamburgers, you can simply prepare the sauce separately in a skillet while the burgers are cooking, and then briefly simmer the burgers in the skillet to coat them with the zesty sauce.

Working time: 10 minutes
Total time: 25 minutes

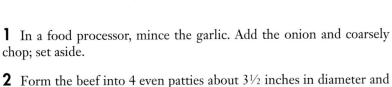

Stovetop Barbecued Burgers

4 Servings

2 cloves garlic	**¼ cup ketchup**
1 medium onion	**2 tablespoons frozen orange juice**
1 pound lean ground beef	**concentrate**
2 teaspoons olive or other	**1 tablespoon chili powder**
vegetable oil	**¼ teaspoon pepper**
1 cup crushed tomatoes	

1 In a food processor, mince the garlic. Add the onion and coarsely chop; set aside.

2 Form the beef into 4 even patties about 3½ inches in diameter and ¾ inch thick.

Step 2

3 In a large skillet, warm the oil over medium-high heat until hot but not smoking. Add the burgers and cook for 5 minutes.

4 Turn the burgers over and cook until browned on the second side but still slightly pink in the center, about 4 minutes. Remove the burgers to a plate and cover loosely to keep warm.

5 Add the garlic-onion mixture to the skillet and cook, stirring, over medium heat until the onion begins to brown, about 5 minutes.

6 Add the tomatoes, ketchup, orange juice concentrate, chili powder and pepper. Bring the mixture to a boil over medium-high heat and boil for 1 minute.

Step 6

7 Return the burgers (and any juices that have accumulated on the plate) to the skillet, baste with some of the sauce, and cook for 1 minute, or until the burgers are heated through.

TIME-SAVERS

■ **Do-ahead:** *The barbecue sauce can be made well ahead.*

Values are approximate per serving: Calories: 341   Protein: 23 gm   Fat: 22 gm
Carbohydrates: 12 gm   Cholesterol: 78 mg   Sodium: 278 mg

Step 7

Ham, White Bean and Sweet Potato Soup

This nourishing dish—made with canned beans and diced ham—is a streamlined version of old-fashioned, long-cooking soups made with dried beans and a ham hock. The sweet potato adds a hint of sweetness and a touch of color, but a white potato could certainly be substituted. And if you cannot easily find canned white beans, check the Spanish and Mexican food shelves for cans labeled "habichuelas blancas."

Working time: 15 minutes
Total time: 30 minutes

Ham, White Bean and Sweet Potato Soup

6 Servings

2½ cups chicken broth
1 cup water
2 cloves garlic, minced or crushed through a press
1 teaspoon Dijon mustard
¼ teaspoon pepper
1 bay leaf

1 can (16 ounces) small white beans
1 medium sweet potato (about 8 ounces)
½ pound ham, preferably smoked ham, such as Black Forest
2 scallions

Step 2

1 In a medium saucepan, bring the chicken broth, water, garlic, mustard, pepper and bay leaf to a boil over medium-high heat.

2 Meanwhile, drain the beans in a colander. Rinse under cold running water and drain well. Peel the sweet potato and cut it into ½-inch dice.

3 Add the beans and sweet potato to the broth and return it to a boil. Reduce the heat to medium-low, cover and simmer, stirring occasionally, until the sweet potato is tender, about 20 minutes.

4 Meanwhile, dice the ham and coarsely chop the scallions.

5 Add the ham and scallions to the soup and cook for 1 minute longer to heat through. Discard the bay leaf before serving.

Step 3

TIME-SAVERS

■ **Do-ahead:** *The sweet potato, ham and scallions can be cut up ahead. The whole soup can be made ahead.*

Values are approximate per serving: Calories: 101 Protein: 10 gm Fat: 3 gm
Carbohydrates: 9 gm Cholesterol: 20 mg Sodium: 887 mg

Step 5

Gingered Pork Cutlets

Ginger, garlic, soy sauce and honey give these sautéed pork slices the flavor of Japanese teriyaki cooking, in which foods are brushed with a savory sauce and broiled or grilled. Since the cutlets are just ¼-inch thick, they pan cook in less than 10 minutes. Serve the pork with steamed white rice and, perhaps, a simple tossed green salad.

Working time: 25 minutes
Total time: 25 minutes

4 Servings

- 5 quarter-size slices (¼ inch thick) fresh ginger, unpeeled
- 3 cloves garlic, minced or crushed through a press
- 3 tablespoons reduced-sodium or regular soy sauce
- 2 tablespoons honey
- 1 pound boneless loin pork chops (about ¼ inch thick)
- 4 scallions
- 1 large red bell pepper
- 2 tablespoons vegetable oil
- 3 tablespoons cornstarch
- ¼ cup beef broth

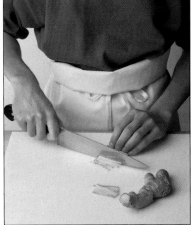

1 Cut 3 of the ginger slices into slivers. Leave the remaining 2 slices whole.

2 In a shallow bowl, combine the slivered ginger, the garlic, soy sauce and honey. Add the pork and toss to thoroughly coat with the marinade.

Step 1

3 Cut the scallions into 1½-inch lengths. Cut the bell pepper into thin strips.

4 In a large skillet, warm 1 tablespoon of the oil over medium-high heat until hot but not smoking. Add the 2 whole ginger slices, the scallions and bell pepper and stir-fry until the vegetables are just wilted, about 3 minutes. Remove the vegetables from the skillet and set aside.

5 Drain the pork slices, reserving the marinade. Place the cornstarch in a shallow bowl and lightly dredge the pork in it, reserving the excess cornstarch.

6 Add the remaining 1 tablespoon oil to the skillet and warm over medium-high heat until hot but not smoking. Add the pork and brown all over, about 3 minutes per side.

Step 4

7 Combine 3 tablespoons of the reserved marinade with 1 teaspoon of the reserved cornstarch. Add the cornstarch mixture to the skillet and bring to a boil; cook, stirring, until slightly thickened, about 1 minute. Stir in the broth and return the vegetables to the pan. Cook for about 1 minute to heat through.

TIME-SAVERS

■ **Do-ahead:** *The ginger and vegetables can be cut up ahead.*

Values are approximate per serving: Calories: 314 Protein: 25 gm Fat: 16 gm
Carbohydrates: 18 gm Cholesterol: 68 mg Sodium: 577 mg

Step 6

Three-Pepper Smothered Minute Steak

▼

True to their name, minute steaks cook very quickly. Here, they are sautéed, then topped with a multicolored toss of quick-braised bell peppers. The low calorie count allows you to fill out the meal with a generous helping of a healthful carbohydrate, such as white rice. Or try "instant" brown rice, which cooks in minutes and supplies a good amount of fiber. A baked potato (microwaved in minutes) is another healthy choice.

Working time: 10 minutes
Total time: 25 minutes

Three-Pepper Smothered Minute Steak

4 Servings

1 medium red bell pepper	**1 teaspoon oregano**
1 medium yellow bell pepper	**¼ teaspoon black pepper**
1 medium green bell pepper	**1 tablespoon olive or other**
1 small onion	**vegetable oil**
½ cup beef broth	**1 minute steak (about ¾ pound)**
2 cloves garlic, minced or crushed	**2 tablespoons water**
through a press	**1 tablespoon cornstarch**

Step 1

1 Cut the bell peppers lengthwise into thin strips. Thinly slice the onion.

2 In a medium saucepan, bring the beef broth, garlic, oregano and black pepper to a boil over medium-high heat. Add the bell peppers and onion. Let return to a boil, then reduce the heat to low, cover and simmer for 5 minutes.

3 Meanwhile, in a medium nonstick skillet, warm the oil over medium-high heat until hot but not smoking. Add the steak and brown all over, about 3 minutes per side. Remove from the heat and cover loosely to keep warm.

Step 2

4 In a small bowl, blend the water and cornstarch. Return the broth and peppers to a boil over medium-high heat. Stir in the cornstarch mixture and cook, stirring, until the broth thickens slightly, 1 to 2 minutes.

5 Cut the steak into serving portions and serve topped with the peppers.

TIME-SAVERS

■ ***Do-ahead:*** *The vegetables can be cut up ahead.*

Values are approximate per serving: Calories: 234 Protein: 18 gm Fat: 15 gm
Carbohydrates: 6 gm Cholesterol: 54 mg Sodium: 151 mg

Step 3

Pork Satay with Dipping Sauce

▼

In Southeast Asia, skewers of grilled meat (called satay or saté) are most commonly eaten as a street-food snack or a restaurant appetizer. But served in more generous portions, these pork satay with a gingered peanut sauce make a delicious and unusual meal. If you have time, place the uncooked pork loin in the freezer for fifteen minutes (not longer); the brief chilling will make it easier to thinly slice the meat.

Working time: 20 minutes
Total time: 30 minutes

Pork Satay with Dipping Sauce

4 Servings

6 quarter-size slices (¼ inch thick) fresh ginger, unpeeled
1 pound boneless pork loin
3 tablespoons reduced-sodium soy sauce
1 tablespoon Oriental sesame oil
2 teaspoons honey
3 cloves garlic, minced or crushed through a press
1 teaspoon ground coriander
¼ cup creamy peanut butter
3 tablespoons chicken broth
1 tablespoon rice wine vinegar or distilled white vinegar
3 tablespoons chopped cilantro (optional)

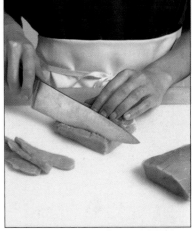

1 Mince the ginger and set aside.

2 Preheat the broiler. Line a broiler pan with foil.

3 Cut the pork loin in half, then cut each half into thin strips. Thread the pork strips onto skewers and place the skewers on the broiler pan.

Step 3

4 In a small bowl, combine the soy sauce, 2 teaspoons of the sesame oil, the honey, garlic, half of the minced ginger and the coriander.

5 Brush the pork with the basting mixture and broil 4 inches from the heat for 5 minutes. Turn the pork over and broil for an additional 4 minutes, or until the pork is cooked through.

6 Meanwhile, in a small bowl, blend the peanut butter, chicken broth, vinegar, remaining 1 teaspoon sesame oil and remaining minced ginger and the chopped cilantro (if using). When the pork is done, stir any pan juices into the peanut dipping sauce. You should have about 3 tablespoons of pan juices; if not, use chicken broth to make up the difference.

Step 3

7 Serve the pork with the dipping sauce on the side.

TIME-SAVERS

■ ***Do-ahead:*** *The basting mixture (Step 4) can be made and the pork threaded on skewers ahead of time. The peanut sauce can be made ahead and the pan juices from cooking the pork stirred in just before serving.*

Step 6

Values are approximate per serving: Calories: 402 Protein: 27 gm Fat: 29 gm
Carbohydrates: 8 gm Cholesterol: 77 mg Sodium: 629 mg

Beefy Tortellini Soup

▼

Cheese-filled tortellini become instant dumplings for this beef soup, which is made by boosting the flavor of canned broth or bouillon with ground beef, vegetables and herbs. Fresh tortellini, which you'll find in the dairy case of the supermarket, cook in about 12 minutes; if you can find only dried tortellini, add them to the soup a few minutes earlier to allow for the slightly longer cooking time.

Working time: 15 minutes
Total time: 30 minutes

Beefy Tortellini Soup

4 Servings

2 medium carrots
1 medium onion
1 tablespoon olive or other
  vegetable oil
2 cloves garlic, minced or crushed
  through a press
¼ pound lean ground beef
2½ cups beef broth
1½ cups water

1 cup crushed tomatoes
1 teaspoon basil
¼ teaspoon pepper
½ pound fresh cheese-filled
  tortellini (about 2 cups)
1 medium zucchini
¼ cup grated Parmesan cheese
  (optional)

Step 3

1 Cut the carrots into ¼-inch slices and set aside. Coarsely chop the onion.

2 In a medium saucepan, warm the oil over medium-high heat until hot but not smoking. Add the onion and garlic and stir-fry until the mixture just begins to brown, about 3 minutes.

3 Crumble in the beef and cook, stirring, until the meat is no longer pink, about 3 minutes.

4 Add the beef broth, water and crushed tomatoes. Cover and bring the mixture to a boil over medium-high heat. Add the carrots, basil and pepper, and cook uncovered, stirring occasionally, for 2 minutes.

5 Add the tortellini and cook until al dente, 10 to 12 minutes or according to package directions.

Step 5

6 Meanwhile, halve the zucchini lengthwise and then cut crosswise into ¼-inch half-rounds. Three minutes before the tortellini are done, add the zucchini to the soup. Continue cooking, uncovered, until the zucchini is crisp-tender. Serve the soup with Parmesan cheese on the side, if desired.

TIME-SAVERS

■ *Microwave tip: In a 3-quart microwave-safe casserole, combine the onion (finely, not coarsely, chopped), thinly sliced carrot, garlic and beef (omit the oil). Cover and cook at 100% for 4 minutes, stirring once to break up the beef. Stir in the beef broth, hot water, crushed tomatoes, basil, pepper and zucchini. Cover and cook at 100% for 8 minutes, or until the liquid boils. Stir in the tortellini. Cook at 50% for 6 minutes, or until the pasta is done.*

■ *Do-ahead: The soup can be made ahead through Step 4; before serving, return the soup to a boil and proceed with Steps 5 and 6.*

Values are approximate per serving: Calories: 332 Protein: 18 gm Fat: 13 gm
Carbohydrates: 37 gm Cholesterol: 52 mg Sodium: 901 mg

Step 6

Broiled Ham Steak with Pineapple and Mustard Glaze

▼

Juicy ham steaks make perfect busy-day dinners. Fully cooked, they need only a short time in the oven or under the broiler to bring out their full flavor. Here, sweet and spicy ingredients are combined to make an attractive topping and tangy glaze; the broiled pineapple provides a traditional sweet counterpoint to the ham's saltiness.

Working time: 10 minutes
Total time: 25 minutes

Broiled Ham Steak with Pineapple and Mustard Glaze

6 Servings

**2 cans (8¼ ounces each)
   unsweetened juice-packed
   pineapple slices**
3 tablespoons dry mustard
1 tablespoon brown sugar

¼ teaspoon ground cloves
¼ teaspoon pepper
**1½-pound ham steak (ready to
   eat)**

1 Preheat the broiler. Line a broiler pan with foil.

2 Drain the pineapple, reserving 4 tablespoons of the juice.

3 In a small bowl, combine the reserved pineapple juice, mustard, sugar, cloves and pepper to make the glaze.

4 Place the ham steak on the broiler pan and brush the top with half of the glaze. Broil 4 inches from the heat for 7 minutes, or until golden.

5 Turn the steak over and brush with half of the remaining glaze. Arrange the pineapple rings on top of the steak and brush them with the remaining glaze.

6 Broil 4 inches from the heat for 7 minutes longer, or until the pineapple is light golden around the edges.

Step 3

Step 4

Step 5

Values are approximate per serving: Calories: 293 Protein: 23 gm Fat: 15 gm
Carbohydrates: 15 gm Cholesterol: 60 mg Sodium: 1533 mg

Lamb Chops with Cucumber-Mint Salsa

▼

A lighter version of the classic roast lamb with mint sauce, these aromatic grilled chops have a double hit of mint: They are basted on the barbecue with minty olive oil, then served with a sweet-hot cucumber-mint relish. Accompany the chops and salsa with baby summer squash. Steam the vegetables indoors, or drizzle with olive oil, enclose them in foil packets and cook them on the grill.

Working time: 15 minutes
Total time: 25 minutes

Lamb Chops with Cucumber-Mint Salsa

4 Servings

⅓ cup (packed) fresh mint leaves or 1 tablespoon dried

2 tablespoons olive or other vegetable oil

4 cloves garlic, minced or crushed through a press

¾ teaspoon salt

½ teaspoon pepper

8 small loin lamb chops (about 2¼ pounds total), well trimmed

1 medium cucumber

2 tablespoons cider vinegar

2 teaspoons sugar

Pinch of cayenne pepper

1 Preheat the broiler or start the charcoal. If broiling, line a broiler pan with foil.

2 In a food processor, finely chop the fresh mint; remove and set aside. (Do not clean the work bowl.)

3 In a small bowl, combine the oil, garlic, half of the mint, ½ teaspoon of the salt and the pepper.

4 Brush the chops with half of the mint oil. (If broiling, place the chops on the broiler pan first.) Broil or grill the chops 4 inches from the heat for 8 minutes.

5 Turn the chops over, brush with the remaining mint oil and broil or grill 4 inches from the heat for 8 minutes for medium-rare; 10 minutes for medium; 12 minutes for well-done.

6 Meanwhile, peel the cucumber. In the uncleaned processor work bowl, very coarsely chop the cucumber.

7 In a medium bowl, combine the cucumber, remaining mint, vinegar, sugar, cayenne and remaining ¼ teaspoon salt.

8 Serve the chops with the cucumber-mint salsa on the side.

TIME-SAVERS

■ *Do-ahead: The mint oil (Steps 2 and 3) and cucumber-mint salsa (Steps 2, 6 and 7) can both be made well ahead.*

Values are approximate per serving: Calories: 291 Protein: 30 gm Fat: 16 gm
Carbohydrates: 6 gm Cholesterol: 92 mg Sodium: 497 mg

Step 3

Step 4

Step 7

Stuffed Zucchini Boats

▼

Just eight ounces of ground beef can stretch to feed four people when it's used to stuff hollowed-out zucchini halves (yellow or crookneck squash could be prepared the same way). The part-skim mozzarella used here is one of the lowest-fat natural cheeses, and is available in chunks, slices and even pre-shredded for convenience. To cut fat, calories and cholesterol still further, substitute ground turkey for the beef.

Working time: 15 minutes
Total time: 30 minutes

Stuffed Zucchini Boats

4 Servings

4 large zucchini (about 2 pounds total)
⅔ cup low-sodium or regular beef broth
2 cloves garlic, minced or crushed through a press
¾ teaspoon basil
¼ teaspoon pepper
½ pound lean ground beef
2 teaspoons cornstarch
1 large or 2 small plum tomatoes
⅓ cup shredded part-skim mozzarella

Step 2

1 Halve the zucchini lengthwise.

2 In a large skillet, bring the broth, garlic, basil and pepper to a boil over medium-high heat. Add the zucchini halves, reduce the heat to low, cover and simmer until barely tender, about 5 minutes.

3 Remove the zucchini and set aside to cool slightly. Measure out and remove ¼ cup of the broth, leaving the remainder in the skillet.

4 Increase the heat under the skillet to medium. Crumble in the ground beef and cook, stirring occasionally to break it up, until the meat is no longer pink, about 5 minutes.

5 Preheat the broiler. Line a baking sheet with foil.

6 Meanwhile, carefully scoop out the zucchini flesh, leaving a ¼-inch-thick shell. Coarsely chop the flesh.

Step 6

7 In a small bowl, combine the reserved ¼ cup of broth with the cornstarch and stir to combine. Bring the beef mixture to a boil over medium-high heat. Add the chopped zucchini and the cornstarch mixture. Cook, stirring, for about 1 minute, or until the liquid has thickened. Remove the skillet from the heat.

8 Coarsely chop the tomatoes and stir them into the beef mixture.

9 Place the zucchini halves on the prepared baking sheet. Dividing evenly, mound the beef mixture into the hollowed-out zucchini and sprinkle with the mozzarella. Broil 4 inches from the heat until the cheese is melted and bubbling, 2 to 3 minutes.

TIME-SAVERS

■ ***Do-ahead:*** *The zucchini can be cooked ahead. The cooked zucchini can also be stuffed ahead and then broiled just before serving.*

Values are approximate per serving: Calories: 222 Protein: 15 gm Fat: 14 gm
Carbohydrates: 10 gm Cholesterol: 48 mg Sodium: 93 mg

Step 9

Chinese Hot Pot

This protein-packed stew is made with ground pork, chick peas and, if desired, tofu. Tofu, or soybean curd, is so high in protein that the Chinese sometimes refer to it as "meat without bones," and its neutral taste readily absorbs the flavors of other ingredients. If you are going to include the tofu in this recipe, try to find the firm kind, which is sold in compact cakes that resemble small ivory-colored pillows.

Working time: 20 minutes
Total time: 30 minutes

Chinese Hot Pot

4 Servings

1 can (19 ounces) chick peas
¼ cup (packed) cilantro sprigs (optional)
5 quarter-size slices (¼ inch thick) fresh ginger, unpeeled
2 teaspoons Oriental sesame oil
3 cloves garlic, minced or crushed through a press
¼ pound lean ground pork
2½ cups chicken broth
1 can (8 ounces) sliced bamboo shoots, drained

1 can (8 ounces) sliced water chestnuts, drained
1 tablespoon reduced-sodium or regular soy sauce
2 drops hot pepper sauce
½ teaspoon red pepper flakes
¼ pound firm tofu (about 1 cake; optional)
2 tablespoons cornstarch
¼ pound fresh or frozen snow peas

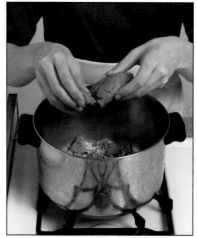

Step 3

1 Drain the chick peas in a colander, rinse under cold running water and drain well. Finely chop the cilantro (if using). Finely chop the ginger.

2 In a large saucepan, warm the sesame oil over medium-high heat until hot but not smoking. Add the ginger and garlic, and stir-fry until fragrant, about 1 minute.

3 Crumble in the ground pork and stir-fry until the meat begins to brown, about 3 minutes.

4 Add the drained chick peas, 2 cups of the chicken broth, the bamboo shoots, water chestnuts, soy sauce, hot pepper sauce and red pepper flakes. Bring the mixture to a boil over medium heat.

5 Meanwhile, cut the tofu (if using) into ½-inch cubes. In a small bowl, blend the cornstarch with the remaining ½ cup chicken broth. If using fresh snow peas, trim the ends and strings.

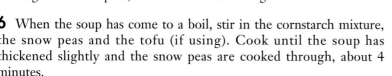

Step 5

6 When the soup has come to a boil, stir in the cornstarch mixture, the snow peas and the tofu (if using). Cook until the soup has thickened slightly and the snow peas are cooked through, about 4 minutes.

7 Stir in the cilantro (if using) and serve hot.

TIME-SAVERS

■ *Do-ahead: The hot pot can be made ahead, but do not stir in the snow peas and tofu until just before serving.*

Values are approximate per serving: Calories: 278   Protein: 13 gm   Fat: 12 gm
Carbohydrates: 30 gm   Cholesterol: 21 mg   Sodium: 942 mg

Step 6

London Broil with Chili Seasonings

▼

London broil is the market name for a number of steaks, including flank and top round, that are best served broiled or grilled and thinly sliced. On the lean side, these steaks also benefit from being basted or marinated (which helps keep the meat juicy) and then carved on the diagonal and against the grain (this cuts across the long fibers of the meat so it seems even more tender).

Working time: 5 minutes
Total time: 25 minutes

London Broil with Chili Seasonings

6 Servings

3 tablespoons olive or other
   vegetable oil
1 tablespoon Worcestershire sauce
3 cloves garlic, minced or crushed
   through a press
¼ cup chopped parsley (optional)
3 tablespoons chili powder

2 teaspoons cumin
2 teaspoons paprika
½ teaspoon salt
¼ teaspoon black pepper
Pinch of cayenne pepper
1½-pound London broil

Step 2

1 Preheat the broiler. Line a broiler pan with foil.

2 In a small bowl, combine the oil, Worcestershire sauce, garlic, parsley (if using), chili powder, cumin, paprika, salt, black pepper and cayenne.

3 Place the steak on the broiler pan and brush with half of the marinade.

4 Broil the steak 4 inches from the heat for 7 minutes.

5 Turn the steak over, brush the other side with the remaining marinade and broil 4 inches from the heat until well browned, about 7 minutes for medium-rare, 9 minutes for medium and 11 minutes for well-done. Let the steak stand for 5 minutes before slicing.

6 To serve, cut the steak into thin slices across the grain and on the diagonal.

Step 3

TIME-SAVERS

■ *Do-ahead: The marinade (Step 2) can be made ahead. The steak can marinate for several hours before being broiled: use three-fourths of the marinade to coat both sides of the steak, then use the remaining marinade for basting the steak as it broils.*

Values are approximate per serving: Calories: 297 Protein: 22 gm Fat: 21 gm
Carbohydrates: 4 gm Cholesterol: 60 mg Sodium: 319 mg

Step 6

Pork Chops with Fresh Cranberry Sauce

Although most supermarkets now carry frozen cranberries year 'round, they are always available fresh at Thanksgiving. To ensure a good supply for your favorite recipes, buy a few bags of cranberries when they're plentiful and store them in your freezer. No special preparation is necessary for freezing, and for most recipes (including this one), you don't even need to thaw them.

Working time: 15 minutes
Total time: 25 minutes

Pork Chops with Fresh Cranberry Sauce

4 Servings

3 tablespoons flour
¼ teaspoon pepper
4 center-cut loin pork chops (½ inch thick, about 1¼ pounds total)
1 tablespoon vegetable oil
1 tablespoon butter

½ cup apple juice
½ cup chicken broth
1 tablespoon brown sugar
1 tablespoon grated orange zest (optional)
1 cup cranberries, fresh or frozen
2 scallions

1 In a shallow bowl, combine the flour and pepper. Lightly dredge the pork chops in the seasoned flour. Reserve the dredging mixture.

2 In a large skillet, warm the oil over medium-high heat until hot but not smoking. Add the chops and cook until browned on both sides, 2 to 3 minutes per side. Remove the chops to a plate and cover loosely to keep warm.

Step 2

3 Add the butter to the skillet and melt over medium heat. Stir in 1 tablespoon of the reserved dredging mixture and stir until the flour has absorbed all of the butter.

4 Stir in the apple juice, broth, brown sugar, orange zest (if using) and cranberries, and bring the mixture to a boil over medium-high heat. Return the pork chops (and any juices that have accumulated on the plate) to the skillet, reduce the heat to medium-low, cover and simmer for 5 minutes.

5 Turn the chops over, cover and simmer another 5 minutes.

6 Meanwhile, coarsely chop the scallions.

7 Stir the scallions into the sauce and serve the chops with some of the cranberry sauce spooned over them.

Step 4

Values are approximate per serving: Calories: 445 Protein: 23 gm Fat: 32 gm
Carbohydrates: 15 gm Cholesterol: 90 mg Sodium: 221 mg

Step 7

Sweet-and-Sour Mustard Scaloppini

Veal scaloppini are boneless veal cutlets that have been pounded until they are very thin. If your market has only the thicker veal cutlets, you can either cook them as they are (allowing a bit more cooking time) or pound them yourself. Place the cutlets between two sheets of plastic wrap and use a meat pounder, mallet or rolling pin to flatten them to about a ⅛-inch thickness.

Working time: 20 minutes
Total time: 20 minutes

Sweet-and-Sour
Mustard Scaloppini

4 Servings

⅓ **cup flour**
½ **teaspoon salt**
¼ **teaspoon pepper**
8 **veal scaloppini (about 1 pound total)**
2 **tablespoons butter**
2 **tablespoons olive or other vegetable oil**
½ **cup beer**

½ **cup chicken broth**
2 **tablespoons spicy brown mustard**
2 **tablespoons brown sugar**
1 **teaspoon dry mustard**
1 **teaspoon thyme**
3 **tablespoons lemon juice**
1½ **teaspoons grated lemon zest (optional)**

Step 2

1 In a shallow bowl, combine the flour, salt and pepper. Dredge the veal lightly in the seasoned flour, reserving the excess.

2 In a large skillet, warm 1 tablespoon of the butter in 1 tablespoon of the oil over medium-high heat until the butter is melted. Add the veal and brown all over, about 2 minutes per side, adding the remaining 1 tablespoon oil to prevent sticking. Remove the veal to a plate and cover loosely to keep warm.

3 Add the remaining 1 tablespoon butter to the skillet and heat until just melted. Stir in the reserved dredging mixture and cook, stirring, until the flour is no longer visible, about 30 seconds.

4 Stir in the beer, chicken broth, spicy brown mustard, sugar, dry mustard and thyme. Bring the mixture to a boil, stirring constantly, and cook until slightly thickened, 1 to 2 minutes.

Step 4

5 Stir in the lemon juice and lemon zest (if using). Return the veal (and any juices that have accumulated on the plate) to the skillet and bring the mixture to a boil over medium-high heat. Reduce the heat to low, cover and simmer until the veal is cooked through, 1 to 2 minutes.

6 Serve the veal topped with the sauce.

Values are approximate per serving: Calories: 324   Protein: 26 gm   Fat: 15 gm
Carbohydrates: 17 gm   Cholesterol: 104 mg   Sodium: 609 mg

Step 5

Skillet-Roasted Steak
with Piquant Sauce

▼

*For a change from broiled or pan-cooked steak, try this skillet-roasting method:
The steaks are seared in an ovenproof skillet to seal in juices and flavor, then
placed in a very hot oven and roasted. The pan juices are then used as the basis for
the piquant sauce, which is cooked in the same skillet. If you can't
find small shell steaks, buy larger ones and cut them in half.*

Working time: 15 minutes
Total time: 25 minutes

Skillet-Roasted Steak
with Piquant Sauce

4 Servings

**2 teaspoons olive or other
vegetable oil**
**4 small shell steaks (about ¾ inch
thick, 1½ pounds total)**
½ cup dry red wine
2 tablespoons tomato paste
½ teaspoon hot pepper sauce

**2 cloves garlic, minced or crushed
through a press**
1 teaspoon fennel seed
½ teaspoon sugar
¼ teaspoon pepper
½ cup beef broth
2 teaspoons cornstarch

1 Preheat the oven to 450°.

2 In a large ovenproof skillet, warm the oil over high heat until hot but not smoking. Add the steaks and sear for 2 minutes per side.

3 Place the skillet in the oven and roast the steaks for 3 minutes.

Step 2

4 Turn the steaks over and roast for an additional 3 minutes, or until medium-rare.

5 Remove the steaks to a plate and cover loosely to keep warm. Add the red wine, tomato paste, hot pepper sauce, garlic, fennel seed, sugar and pepper to the skillet, and bring the mixture to a boil over medium-high heat.

6 Meanwhile, in a small bowl, blend the beef broth and cornstarch. Add the cornstarch-broth mixture to the skillet. Cook, stirring, until the sauce thickens slightly, about 2 minutes.

7 Return the steaks (and any juices that have accumulated on the plate) to the skillet. Turn the steaks to coat them with the sauce.

Step 5

8 Serve the steaks topped with sauce.

Values are approximate per serving: Calories: 427 Protein: 33 gm Fat: 28 gm
Carbohydrates: 5 gm Cholesterol: 114 mg Sodium: 277 mg

Step 7

Beef Tacos
with Fresh Salsa

▼

Fresh, hot, homemade Mexican food is guaranteed to get the family's attention at dinnertime. For this hearty main dish, tacos stuffed with a beef filling are topped with a lively bell pepper-tomato salsa. Optional additions include shredded Cheddar or jack cheese, guacamole and sour cream. For the braver palates at the table, you can also serve a bowl of chopped jalapeño peppers and bottled hot sauces.

Working time: 30 minutes
Total time: 30 minutes

Beef Tacos
with Fresh Salsa

4 Servings

1 small onion
3 tablespoons olive or other
   vegetable oil
2 cloves garlic, minced or crushed
   through a press
½ pound lean ground beef
Half a 14½-ounce can stewed
   tomatoes, drained
Half a 4-ounce can of chopped mild
   green chilies, drained
2 tablespoons chili powder
1½ teaspoons cumin
1 teaspoon oregano

Pinch of cayenne pepper
1 small green bell pepper
1 medium fresh tomato
3 scallions
¼ cup cilantro sprigs (optional)
2 tablespoons red wine vinegar or
   cider vinegar
¼ teaspoon black pepper
3 drops hot pepper sauce
2 cups shredded Romaine lettuce
   (about 6 leaves)
12 taco shells

Step 4

1 Coarsely chop the onion.

2 In a large skillet, warm 1 tablespoon of the oil over medium-high heat until hot but not smoking. Add the onion and garlic and cook until the mixture begins to brown, 3 to 5 minutes.

3 Crumble in the beef and cook, breaking up the beef with a spoon, for 2 to 3 minutes.

4 Add the stewed tomatoes, green chilies, chili powder, cumin, ¼ teaspoon of the oregano and the cayenne, breaking up the tomatoes with a spoon. Reduce the heat to low, cover and simmer while you prepare the remaining ingredients.

5 Coarsely chop the bell pepper, fresh tomato and scallions. Finely chop the cilantro (if using).

Step 6

6 In a small bowl, combine the bell pepper, tomato, scallions, cilantro, the remaining 2 tablespoons oil, the vinegar, the remaining ¾ teaspoon oregano, the black pepper and hot pepper sauce.

7 Shred the lettuce.

8 Fill each taco shell with ¼ cup of the beef mixture and top with shredded lettuce. Top the tacos with salsa or serve it on the side.

TIME-SAVERS

■ **Do-ahead:** *The beef mixture and salsa can both be made ahead.*

Values are approximate per serving: Calories: 446 Protein: 12 gm Fat: 29 gm
Carbohydrates: 36 gm Cholesterol: 43 mg Sodium: 318 mg

Step 8

Pork Chops with Gingered Pears

▼

Ground ginger perks up the flavor of both the pork and the pears in this sophisticated autumnal entrée. Because the chops are garnished with unpeeled pear slices, a Red Bartlett would be an especially attractive choice for this recipe. In a pinch you can even use canned pears, although they should be well drained first and they should not be sautéed or they will fall apart.

Working time: 20 minutes
Total time: 25 minutes

Pork Chops with Gingered Pears

4 Servings

3 tablespoons lemon juice
3 tablespoons Dijon mustard
1 teaspoon thyme
4 loin pork chops (½ inch thick, about 1½ pounds total)
1 large pear, preferably Red Bartlett, unpeeled

1 tablespoon butter
¼ cup apple juice
2 teaspoons grated lemon zest (optional)
½ teaspoon ground ginger
2 scallions

1 Preheat the broiler. Line a broiler pan with foil.

2 In a small bowl, combine the lemon juice, mustard and thyme.

3 Place the chops on the broiler pan and brush them with half of the lemon-mustard mixture. Broil the chops 4 inches from the heat for 5 minutes.

Step 3

4 Turn the chops over and brush them with the remaining lemon-mustard mixture. Broil for 7 minutes longer, or until the chops are cooked through.

5 Meanwhile, core the pear and cut it lengthwise into about 16 thin slices.

6 In a medium skillet, warm the butter over medium heat until the butter is melted. Add the pear slices and cook until browned on both sides, about 1 minute. Add the apple juice, lemon zest (if using) and ginger, and bring the mixture to a boil.

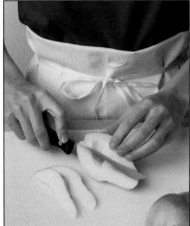
Step 5

7 Remove the skillet from the heat, remove 8 pear slices for garnish, if desired, and set aside. Mash the remaining pears with a potato masher or wooden spoon. Return the skillet to low heat and let the excess moisture cook off while you finish broiling the chops; stir occasionally to prevent sticking.

8 Finely chop the scallions. Serve the chops with the pear sauce and garnished with pear slices and chopped scallions.

TIME-SAVERS

■ *Do-ahead: The lemon-mustard mixture (Step 2) can be made ahead. The pear sauce can be made ahead and gently reheated.*

Step 7

Values are approximate per serving: Calories: 391 Protein: 27 gm Fat: 25 gm
Carbohydrates: 13 gm Cholesterol: 102 mg Sodium: 438 mg

Red Snapper with Toasted Almonds (page 229)

CHAPTER 4
SEAFOOD

Swordfish Skewers
with Garlic-Lime Marinade

▼

Swordfish is great for grilling: The firmness and density of a thick swordfish steak (almost more like meat than fish) makes it easy to cut into generous chunks that won't fall off the skewers. You really should not substitute any other type of fish in this recipe, except perhaps monkfish, which is also meaty and firm. If you have time, marinate the swordfish in the basting mixture for an hour before grilling.

Working time: 20 minutes
Total time: 30 minutes

Swordfish Skewers with Garlic-Lime Marinade

4 Servings

1 large or 2 small limes
4 tablespoons olive or other vegetable oil
2 tablespoons tomato paste
2 teaspoons dry mustard
4 cloves garlic, minced or crushed through a press

1 teaspoon salt
½ teaspoon sugar
½ teaspoon black pepper
1 pound swordfish
1 large red onion
1 large yellow or green bell pepper
12 cherry tomatoes

1 Preheat the broiler or start the charcoal. If broiling, line a broiler pan with foil.

2 Grate the lime zest and measure out 2 teaspoons. Juice the lime and measure out 3 tablespoons.

Step 4

3 In a small bowl, combine the lime zest, lime juice, olive oil, tomato paste, dry mustard, garlic, salt, sugar and black pepper.

4 Cut the swordfish into 24 equal pieces. Cut the onion in half and then cut each half into quarters. Cut the bell pepper into 16 pieces about 1 inch square.

5 Dividing equally, thread the swordfish, onions, bell pepper and cherry tomatoes on 8 skewers.

6 Place the skewers on the grill or on the prepared broiler pan and brush with half the basting mixture. Grill or broil 4 inches from the heat for 5 minutes.

7 Turn the skewers over and brush with the remaining basting mixture. Grill or broil until the fish is firm and cooked through, about 5 minutes longer.

Step 5

TIME-SAVERS

■ **Microwave tip:** *To ensure tenderness, you can partially cook the bell pepper and onion before grilling them. Cut the vegetables up and place them on a microwave-safe plate. Cover them with a dampened paper towel and cook at 100% for 2 to 3 minutes, stirring once.*

■ **Do-ahead:** *The basting mixture (Step 3) can be made and the fish and vegetables cut up ahead.*

Values are approximate per serving: Calories: 304 Protein: 24 gm Fat: 19 gm
Carbohydrates: 10 gm Cholesterol: 44 mg Sodium: 722 mg

Step 6

Pecan-Crusted Snapper
with Scallions

▼

Even people who don't like fish may enjoy this unusual combination, in which the sweet, toasty flavor of pecans is partnered with the richness of red snapper. The fish is first dredged in flour, then dipped in egg, and finally coated with a mixture of scallions and chopped pecans; the double dredging forms a crust that seals in the juices as the fish cooks. Serve the snapper with a mild, sweet vegetable, such as corn.

Working time: 15 minutes
Total time: 15 minutes

Pecan-Crusted Snapper with Scallions

4 Servings

1 scallion
½ cup chopped pecans (about 2 ounces)
2 tablespoons fine unseasoned breadcrumbs
¼ cup flour
1 teaspoon salt
½ teaspoon pepper

1 egg
1 tablespoon milk
4 red snapper fillets (about 1 pound total) or other firm-fleshed white fish
About 1 tablespoon butter
1 tablespoon vegetable oil

Step 3

1 Mince the scallion. Finely chop the pecans.

2 In a shallow bowl, combine the scallion, pecans and breadcrumbs. In another shallow bowl, combine the flour, salt and pepper. In a third shallow bowl, beat the egg and milk together.

3 Dredge the fish first in the flour mixture, then in the egg and finally in the pecan mixture.

Step 3

4 In a large skillet, preferably nonstick, warm 1 tablespoon of the butter in the oil over medium-high heat until the butter is melted. Add the fish and cook for 3 minutes, or until golden on the bottom.

5 Carefully turn the fish and cook, adding a little more butter if necessary to prevent sticking, for 3 minutes longer, or until golden on the second side and the fish just flakes when tested with a fork.

TIME-SAVERS

■ **Do-ahead:** *The dredging mixtures can be prepared ahead.*

Step 5

Values are approximate per serving: Calories: 327 Protein: 27 gm Fat: 19 gm
Carbohydrates: 12 gm Cholesterol: 104 mg Sodium: 693 mg

Foil-Baked Sole and Vegetables with Herb Butter

▼

This foil-sealed baking method is a busy cook's dream come true. The packets can be made up in advance and refrigerated until dinner time, and they need no tending as they bake, since the herbed butter bastes both the fish and vegetables. You might like to keep some flavored butter on hand; it's delicious on any kind of fish, vegetables or boiled potatoes. Just make a double batch and freeze half.

Working time: 15 minutes
Total time: 30 minutes

Foil-Baked Sole and Vegetables with Herb Butter

4 Servings

4 scallions
1 large carrot
1 stalk celery
4 fillets of sole (about 1½ pounds total)
⅓ cup butter, at room temperature
3 tablespoons chopped parsley (optional)

1 clove garlic, minced or crushed through a press
½ teaspoon tarragon
¼ teaspoon salt
¼ teaspoon pepper

1 Preheat the oven to 425°. Cut four 12-inch squares of foil.

2 Coarsely chop the scallions. Cut the carrot and celery into thin slices.

3 Place one fish fillet in the center of each sheet of foil. Dividing equally, sprinkle the scallions, carrot and celery on top of the fish.

4 In a small bowl, beat together the butter, parsley (if using), garlic, tarragon, salt and pepper. Divide the herb butter equally among the 4 packets.

5 Bring the long sides of foil together and fold over as you would to wrap a sandwich. Fold in the ends to seal the packets.

6 Place the foil packets on a baking sheet and bake for 12 minutes, or until the fish is opaque throughout and flakes when tested with a fork.

7 Remove the fish and vegetables to individual dinner plates, being sure to pour any butter and juices from the packet on top of the fish.

TIME-SAVERS

■ *Microwave tip: Prepare the ingredients as above, placing the fish in one layer a microwave-safe baking dish and omitting the foil. Cover the dish with plastic wrap, vented at one corner, and cook at 100% for 7 minutes, rotating the dish once. Let stand, covered, for 3 minutes.*

■ *Do-ahead: The herb butter (Step 4) can be made ahead. The foil packets can be assembled, sealed and refrigerated until time to bake.*

Values are approximate per serving: Calories: 307 Protein: 33 gm Fat: 17 gm
Carbohydrates: 4 gm Cholesterol: 123 mg Sodium: 446 mg

Step 3

Step 4

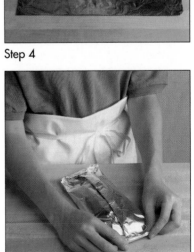

Step 5

Grilled Salmon with Green Sauce

▼

A classic companion for rich, meaty salmon is an intensely herbal "sauce verte," or green sauce. Velvety green sauces can use any of a variety of herbs and greens; this version is made with a combination of fresh dill, basil and parsley, with spinach added for richer color. You could also try adding a small amount of watercress for a peppery kick. Serve the fish with a green salad and herbed garlic bread.

Working time: 15 minutes
Total time: 25 minutes

Grilled Salmon
with Green Sauce

4 Servings

3 tablespoons olive or other vegetable oil
2 tablespoons Dijon mustard
2 tablespoons lemon juice
2 teaspoons grated lemon zest (optional)
3 cloves garlic, minced or crushed through a press
½ teaspoon salt

¼ teaspoon pepper
¼ cup (packed) fresh basil leaves
¼ cup (packed) dill sprigs
¼ cup (packed) parsley sprigs
¼ pound spinach
¼ cup plain yogurt
4 salmon steaks (about ½ pound each)

Step 2

1 Preheat the broiler or start the charcoal. If broiling, line a broiler pan with foil.

2 In a small bowl, blend the oil, mustard, lemon juice, lemon zest (if using), garlic, salt and pepper. Measure out 1 tablespoon of the flavored oil to use as a basting mixture for the salmon; set aside.

3 In a food processor, mince the basil, dill and parsley. Add the spinach and purée. Add the yogurt and blend. With the machine running, drizzle in the flavored oil until the mixture thickens to mayonnaise consistency. Refrigerate until ready to serve.

Step 3

4 Lightly brush the salmon steaks with half of the basting mixture. Grill or broil 4 inches from the heat for 6 minutes. Turn the steaks over, brush with the remaining basting mixture and grill or broil until the fish just flakes when tested with a fork, about 6 minutes.

5 Serve the salmon with the green sauce on the side.

TIME-SAVERS

■ ***Do-ahead:*** *The basting mixture (Step 2) and the green sauce (Steps 2 and 3) can both be made ahead.*

Step 4

Values are approximate per serving: Calories: 411 Protein: 42 gm Fat: 24 gm
Carbohydrates: 6 gm Cholesterol: 111 mg Sodium: 625 mg

Broiled Swordfish with Tomato, Basil and Lemon

▼

If you make this broiled swordfish during the summer and have access to fresh basil, by all means use it (about 1 tablespoon minced) in place of the dried basil in the basting sauce. And in the winter, a season known for its flavorless tomatoes, you might want to use a well drained canned plum tomato instead of the fresh tomato called for.

Working time: 20 minutes
Total time: 20 minutes

Broiled Swordfish with Tomato, Basil and Lemon

4 Servings

3 tablespoons Dijon mustard
2 tablespoons lemon juice
2 tablespoons olive or other
  vegetable oil
2 tablespoons grated Parmesan
  cheese
1 teaspoon basil

¾ teaspoon salt
¼ teaspoon pepper
4 swordfish steaks (½ inch thick,
  about 2 pounds total)
1 small tomato
3 tablespoons chopped parsley
  (optional)

Step 3

1 Preheat the broiler. Line a baking sheet with foil.

2 Make the basting sauce: In a small bowl, stir together the mustard, lemon juice, olive oil, Parmesan, basil, salt and pepper.

3 Place the swordfish steaks on the prepared baking sheet and brush them lightly with some of the basting sauce.

4 Broil the fish 4 inches from the heat until opaque on top, 3 to 4 minutes.

5 Meanwhile, coarsely chop the tomato and parsley (if using) and add them to the remaining basting sauce.

Step 5

6 Turn the fish steaks and spoon the tomato-basting sauce mixture over them. Bake until the fish is firm and just flakes when tested with a fork, 3 to 4 minutes longer.

TIME-SAVERS

■ **Do-ahead:** *The basting sauce can be made ahead.*

Values are approximate per serving: Calories: 337   Protein: 41 gm   Fat: 16 gm
Carbohydrates: 3 gm   Cholesterol: 81 mg   Sodium: 981 mg

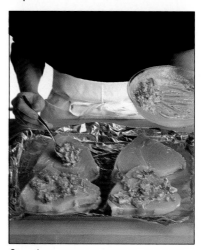

Step 6

Red Snapper with Spicy Orange Sauce

▼

*This simple dish can be made with any firm-fleshed white fish,
although it will be easier to pan-fry if you can get a type that comes with skin
on the fillets, such as striped bass, tilefish, grouper or sea bass. Accompany
this entrée with steamed green beans, crusty peasant bread and perhaps a tossed
salad dressed with vinaigrette spiked with a touch of chili powder.*

Working time: 15 minutes
Total time: 15 minutes

Red Snapper with Spicy Orange Sauce

4 Servings

2 red snapper fillets (¾ inch thick, 1 pound total)	4 tablespoons butter, softened to room temperature
2 tablespoons flour	1 tablespoon frozen orange juice concentrate
¾ teaspoon salt	
⅜ teaspoon pepper	1 teaspoon chili powder
1 tablespoon olive or other vegetable oil	2 tablespoons chopped parsley (optional)

Step 2

1 Cut each fish fillet in half to make 4 equal servings.

2 In a shallow bowl, combine the flour, ½ teaspoon of the salt and ¼ teaspoon of the pepper. Dredge the fish lightly with the seasoned flour.

3 In a large skillet, preferably nonstick, warm the oil over medium-high heat until hot but not smoking. Add the fish and pan-fry, turning once, until the fish flakes easily when tested with a fork, 3 to 4 minutes per side.

Step 3

4 Meanwhile, make the spicy orange sauce: In a small bowl, blend the butter, orange juice concentrate, chili powder, the remaining ¼ teaspoon salt and ⅛ teaspoon pepper.

5 Transfer the fish to individual dinner plates and top each serving with 1 tablespoon of the spicy orange sauce. Sprinkle with the parsley, if desired.

TIME-SAVERS

■ *Microwave tip: There is no real way to approximate pan-frying in the microwave. The following instructions will produce a fish that is more poached than fried, but because it omits the oil and flour, it will also be lower in calories. Arrange the fish in a shallow microwave-safe baking dish. Season with the salt and pepper. Omit the flour and oil. Cook, loosely covered, at 100% for 3 to 5 minutes, rotating the dish once. Make the spicy orange sauce as instructed above.*

■ *Do-ahead: The spicy orange butter sauce can be made well ahead. If desired, double or triple the ingredients for the flavored butter sauce and freeze the extra for later.*

Values are approximate per serving: Calories: 269 Protein: 24 gm Fat: 17 gm Carbohydrates: 5 gm Cholesterol: 73 mg Sodium: 608 mg

Step 4

Herb-Coated Salmon

To preserve the juiciness and flavor of these small, thick salmon fillets, the fish is covered with a mixture of scallions, parsley, garlic, oil, lemon zest and tarragon. (For a variation, try dill instead of tarragon in the herb coating.) Steamed vegetables or tiny new potatoes, tossed with a little tarragon-scented butter, are good accompaniments.

Working time: 10 minutes
Total time: 25 minutes

Herb-Coated Salmon

4 Servings

2 cloves garlic
¼ cup (packed) sprigs of parsley
4 scallions
2 teaspoons grated lemon zest
   (optional)
1 tablespoon olive or other
   vegetable oil

1 teaspoon tarragon
½ teaspoon salt
¼ teaspoon pepper
4 small salmon fillets (¾ to 1 inch
   thick, about 1 pound total)
2 tablespoons lemon juice

Step 2

1 Preheat the oven to 425°. Line a baking sheet with foil and lightly grease the foil.

2 In a food processor, finely chop the garlic. Add the parsley and finely chop. Add the scallions and pulse briefly until they are just chopped.

3 Transfer the mixture to a bowl and stir in the lemon zest (if using), the oil, tarragon, salt and pepper.

4 Place the salmon skin-side down on the prepared baking sheet. Coat the fish with the herb mixture.

5 Bake for about 15 minutes, or until the salmon just flakes when tested with a fork.

6 Sprinkle the fish with the lemon juice before serving.

Step 3

TIME-SAVERS

■ *Microwave tip: Arrange the salmon in a single layer in a shallow microwave-safe baking dish. Cover the salmon with the herb mixture. Loosely cover with waxed paper and cook at 100% for 5 minutes, rotating the dish once, until the fish just flakes when tested with a fork.*

■ *Do-ahead: The herb mixture (Steps 2 and 3) can be made ahead.*

Step 4

Values are approximate per serving: Calories: 201   Protein: 23 gm   Fat: 11 gm
Carbohydrates: 2 gm   Cholesterol: 62 mg   Sodium: 328 mg

Louisiana-Style Fish Cakes with Quick Rémoulade Sauce

▼

A classic rémoulade sauce for seafood is made by slowly whisking oil, drop by drop, into beaten eggs. The resulting mayonnaise is then seasoned with mustard, chopped capers and pickles, herbs and anchovy paste. This quick version is a simple blend of bottled mayonnaise, mustard, pickle relish and tarragon; it's a perfect complement to the slightly peppery fish-and-crab cakes. Serve the cakes on their own or in a sandwich.

Working time: 20 minutes
Total time: 20 minutes

Louisiana-Style Fish Cakes with Quick Rémoulade Sauce

4 Servings

½ **pound flounder fillet or other firm-fleshed white fish**
3 **tablespoons olive or other vegetable oil**
1 **bunch scallions (6 to 8)**
1 **can (6 ounces) lump crabmeat, drained**
2 **eggs, lightly beaten**

5 **tablespoons mayonnaise**
5 **tablespoons Dijon mustard**
1 **cup fine unseasoned breadcrumbs**
¼ **teaspoon black pepper**
Pinch of cayenne pepper
2 **tablespoons butter**
½ **cup pickle relish**
1¼ **teaspoons tarragon**

Step 3

1 Preheat the oven to 375°. Line a baking pan with foil. Place the flounder on the pan and brush with 1 tablespoon of the oil. Bake until opaque throughout, about 8 minutes. Remove and let cool slightly.

2 Meanwhile, coarsely chop the scallions.

3 In a medium bowl, combine the crabmeat with the eggs, 2 table-spoons of the mayonnaise, 2 tablespoons of the mustard, ½ cup of the breadcrumbs, the pepper and cayenne. Stir in the scallions.

4 Flake the flounder and combine it with the crabmeat mixture.

5 Form the mixture into patties about 3½ inches in diameter and ½ inch thick and dredge in the remaining ½ cup breadcrumbs.

6 In a medium skillet, warm 1 tablespoon of the butter in 1 table-spoon of the oil over medium-high heat until the butter melts. Add the fish cakes and fry until golden all over, 2 to 3 minutes per side, turning carefully. Add the remaining butter and oil if necessary.

Step 4

7 Make the rémoulade sauce: In a small bowl, combine the remain-ing 3 tablespoons mayonnaise, 3 tablespoons mustard, the pickle relish and tarragon.

8 Serve the fish cakes with the rémoulade sauce on the side.

TIME-SAVERS

■ *Microwave tip: To cook the flounder, arrange the fillet in a shallow microwave-safe baking dish. Cover loosely with plastic wrap and cook at 100% for 3 minutes, or until opaque throughout.*

■ *Do-ahead: The flounder can be baked and the rémoulade sauce (Step 7) made ahead. The fish cakes can be formed ahead, or even sautéed and then served at room temperature.*

Values are approximate per serving: Calories: 564 Protein: 27 gm Fat: 36 gm
Carbohydrates: 34 gm Cholesterol: 198 mg Sodium: 1341 mg

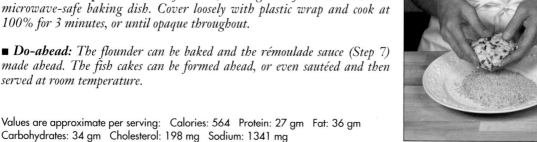
Step 5

Sautéed Sesame Fish

▼

The sesame seeds add a rich, nutty taste to this simple sautéed fish. You can use any firm-fleshed white fish in place of the tilefish, and preferably a type of fish that comes in steak form, such as haddock or cod. Serve with a fresh relish (a sort of mayonnaiseless tartar sauce) of finely chopped tomato and green bell pepper mixed with a small amount of lemon juice.

Working time: 20 minutes
Total time: 20 minutes

Sautéed Sesame Fish

4 Servings

¼ cup flour
1 teaspoon salt
¼ teaspoon pepper
**Four tilefish steaks (¾ to 1 inch
    thick, about 2 pounds total)**
⅔ cup fine, dried breadcrumbs
¼ cup sesame seeds

1 egg
1 tablespoon milk
2 tablespoons butter
2 tablespoons vegetable oil
Lemon wedges and parsley sprigs
    (optional)

Step 2

1 In a bowl, combine the flour, salt and pepper. Dredge the fish lightly in the seasoned flour.

2 In a shallow bowl, combine the breadcrumbs and sesame seeds. In another shallow bowl, beat the egg with the milk until blended.

3 Dip the fish into the egg mixture, then into the breadcrumb mixture, turning to coat the fish completely.

4 In a large skillet, melt the butter in the oil over medium-high heat. When the butter and oil are hot but not smoking, add the fish steaks and cook them until golden brown, about 5 minutes on each side.

5 Serve the fish hot, garnished with lemon wedges and parsley sprigs if desired.

Step 3

TIME-SAVERS

■ ***Do-ahead:*** *The dredging mixtures can be assembled ahead of time.*

Values are approximate per serving: Calories: 476 Protein: 45 gm Fat: 24 gm
Carbohydrates: 19 gm Cholesterol: 43 mg Sodium: 678 mg

Step 3

Swordfish Piccata

▼

This quick, lemony swordfish sauté is a new incarnation of the classic veal or chicken piccata. Sturdy swordfish stands up to gentle sautéing, but do be careful; you can't turn and toss it quite so vigorously as you would veal or chicken. This is a dish worthy of a fresh lemon; the flavorful zest adds an extra dimension to the lemony sauce. Serve the swordfish with a simple cucumber and onion salad.

Working time: 10 minutes
Total time: 15 minutes

Swordfish Piccata

4 Servings

3 large shallots or 1 small onion
1 pound swordfish steaks (about
   ¾ inch thick)
¼ cup flour
½ teaspoon salt
¼ teaspoon pepper
2 tablespoons butter
2 tablespoons olive or other
   vegetable oil

2 cloves garlic, minced or crushed
   through a press
⅓ cup chicken broth
2 tablespoons lemon juice
¼ cup chopped fresh dill or
   1 tablespoon dried
1 tablespoon grated lemon zest
   (optional)

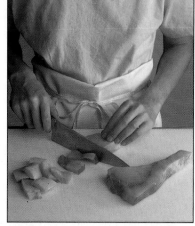

Step 1

1 Halve the shallots or quarter the onion. Cut the swordfish steaks into ½-inch-wide strips.

2 In a plastic or paper bag, combine the flour, salt and pepper, and shake to mix. Add the swordfish and shake to coat lightly. Remove the fish and set aside.

3 In a large skillet, preferably nonstick, warm the butter in the oil over medium-high heat until the butter is melted. Add the shallots (or onion) and garlic, and sauté until the shallots are translucent, about 3 minutes.

4 Add the swordfish strips, and cook, turning them carefully, for 4 minutes.

5 Stir in the chicken broth, lemon juice, dill and lemon zest (if using). Bring the mixture to a boil, remove from the heat and serve hot.

Step 4

TIME-SAVERS

■ **Do-ahead:** *The vegetables and fish can be cut up ahead.*

Step 5

Values are approximate per serving: Calories: 291   Protein: 24 gm   Fat: 17 gm
Carbohydrates: 9 gm   Cholesterol: 60 mg   Sodium: 520 mg

Flounder with Lemon Cream

▼

*While its luxurious texture and heady lemon flavor might convince you that
it is in a culinary class with Hollandaise or Béarnaise, the lemon cream sauce used
here is far simpler to make: Heavy cream is gradually beaten into a mixture
of lemon juice, mustard and tarragon until it forms a soft whipped cream. Be
careful not to overbeat, however, or the sauce may curdle.*

Working time: 10 minutes
Total time: 15 minutes

Flounder with Lemon Cream

4 Servings

2 tablespoons butter
¼ cup lemon juice
1 tablespoon grated lemon zest
  (optional)
1 teaspoon tarragon
½ teaspoon salt
½ teaspoon pepper

4 small flounder fillets (about
  1¼ pounds total) or other
  firm-fleshed white fish, such as
  sole or snapper
1 teaspoon Dijon mustard
½ teaspoon dry mustard
½ cup heavy cream

1 Preheat the broiler. Line a broiler pan with foil.

2 Melt the butter on the stovetop or in the microwave. In a small bowl, combine the melted butter, 2 tablespoons of the lemon juice, 1 teaspoon of the lemon zest (if using), ½ teaspoon of the tarragon, the salt and pepper.

Step 3

3 Place the fish on the prepared broiler pan. Brush the lemon-butter mixture over the fish. Broil the fish 4 inches from the heat for about 7 minutes, or until the fish is cooked through and just flakes when tested with a fork.

4 Meanwhile, in a mixer bowl, combine the remaining 2 tablespoons lemon juice, 2 teaspoons lemon zest (if using), ½ teaspoon tarragon, the Dijon mustard and dry mustard.

5 Gradually beat the cream into the mixture in a thin stream. Continue beating until the cream forms soft peaks. Be careful not to overbeat, as the lemon juice makes the cream more susceptible to curdling.

6 Serve the fish topped with a dollop of the lemon cream.

Step 4

TIME-SAVERS

■ **Do-ahead:** *The lemon-butter mixture (Step 2) can be made ahead.*

Values are approximate per serving: Calories: 290   Protein: 28 gm   Fat: 19 gm
Carbohydrates: 2 gm   Cholesterol: 124 mg   Sodium: 499 mg

Step 5

Red Snapper with Toasted Almonds

▼

Toasted almonds add a note of elegance to fish dishes, and although you can certainly skip this step if you're short on time, the rich flavor and crunchy texture of the nuts make it worth the effort. The method given here is for toasting almonds in a dry skillet, but they can also be toasted on a baking sheet in the oven (at 375° for about 10 minutes) or in a toaster oven (same time and temperature as a conventional oven).

Working time: 15 minutes
Total time: 30 minutes

Red Snapper with Toasted Almonds

4 Servings

⅓ cup sliced almonds
4 scallions
3 tablespoons flour
½ teaspoon salt
¼ teaspoon pepper
1¾ pounds red snapper fillets, or
other firm-fleshed white fish

3 tablespoons butter
1 tablespoon vegetable oil
2 cloves garlic, minced or crushed
through a press

1 Toast the almonds in a large ungreased skillet over medium heat, shaking constantly until golden, about 5 minutes. Remove the almonds from the pan and set aside. Coarsely chop the scallions and set aside.

Step 1

2 In a shallow bowl, combine the flour, salt and pepper. Lightly dredge the snapper fillets in the seasoned flour.

3 In the same large skillet, melt 1 tablespoon of the butter in the oil over medium-high heat until the butter is melted. Add the fillets and sauté until golden brown and cooked through, about 4 minutes per side. Remove the fish to a plate and cover loosely to keep warm.

4 Add the remaining 2 tablespoons butter to the skillet. Add the scallions and garlic and sauté until the scallions are just limp, about 1 minute. Add the almonds and cook for another minute or so.

Step 3

5 Serve the fish topped with the almonds and scallions.

TIME-SAVERS

■ **Do-ahead:** *The almonds can be toasted ahead.*

Values are approximate per serving: Calories: 379 Protein: 43 gm Fat: 19 gm
Carbohydrates: 7 gm Cholesterol: 97 mg Sodium: 490 mg

Step 4

Sea Bass with Lime-Ginger Sauce

A basting sauce made with soy sauce, ginger, lime juice and zest gives an Asian flavor to tender, white sea bass fillets. The same mixture can also be used as a dipping sauce for the cooked fish. You will need a fresh lime for this recipe; bottled lime juice just doesn't have the special tang of fresh juice and zest. Serve the fish with a lightly sautéed, crisp-tender green vegetable, such as snow peas or sugar snap peas.

Working time: 10 minutes
Total time: 20 minutes

Sea Bass with Lime-Ginger Sauce

4 Servings

1 lime
3 quarter-size slices (¼ inch thick) fresh ginger, unpeeled
3 tablespoons reduced-sodium or regular soy sauce
1 tablespoon vegetable oil
2 cloves garlic, minced or crushed through a press

¼ teaspoon red pepper flakes
¼ teaspoon black pepper
1¼ pounds sea bass fillets or other firm-fleshed white fish, such as snapper or scrod

1 Preheat the broiler. Line a broiler pan with foil and grease it lightly.

2 Grate the zest from the lime (there should be about 2 teaspoons). Juice the lime. Cut the ginger into thin slivers.

Step 2

3 In a small bowl, combine the lime zest, lime juice, ginger, soy sauce, oil, garlic, red pepper flakes and black pepper.

4 Place the fish skin-side up on the prepared broiler pan. Drizzle the fish evenly with some of the sauce and broil 4 inches from the heat for about 9 minutes, or until the flesh is opaque and just flakes when tested with a fork.

5 Serve the remaining sauce on the side.

Step 2

TIME-SAVERS

■ *Microwave tip: Although the amount of time saved is not great, cooking this dish in the microwave keeps the kitchen cool in hot weather. Arrange the fillets in a shallow microwave-safe baking dish, with the thicker portions of the fillets toward the rim of the dish. Drizzle some of the basting sauce over the fish and cook, loosely covered, at 100% for 6 minutes, or until the fish is tender, rotating the dish once. Serve with the remaining marinade.*

Values are approximate per serving: Calories: 181 Protein: 27 gm Fat: 6 gm
Carbohydrates: 3 gm Cholesterol: 58 mg Sodium: 547 mg

Step 4

Paella Salad

In a traditional paella—one of the best known culinary creations of Spain—the rice gets its rich golden color from saffron, the world's costliest spice. Here, the more economical turmeric (a spice used in curry powder) is used to give the rice its traditional yellow color. For a more authentic paella flavor, use ½ teaspoon of saffron—preferably threads, not powdered saffron.

Working time: 40 minutes
Total time: 30 minutes

Paella Salad

4 Servings

2 cups chicken broth
2 cloves garlic, minced or crushed
  through a press
2 teaspoons turmeric
½ teaspoon black pepper
1 cup raw rice
¾ pound medium shrimp
¼ pound ham, unsliced
1 large green bell pepper

1 medium red bell pepper
1 medium red onion
¼ cup chopped parsley (optional)
3 tablespoons olive or other
  vegetable oil
2 tablespoons lemon juice
1¼ teaspoons grated lemon zest
  (optional)

1 In a large skillet, bring the chicken broth, garlic, turmeric and black pepper to a boil over medium-high heat. Add the rice, reduce the heat to medium-low, cover and simmer for 15 minutes.

Step 2

2 Meanwhile, shell and devein the shrimp. Cut the shrimp into smaller pieces, if desired. Cut the ham into ½-inch cubes. Cut the green bell pepper into thin strips. Coarsely chop the red bell pepper. Cut the onion crosswise into thin rings.

3 Add the shrimp to the rice and cook for 5 minutes, or until the shrimp is cooked through and the rice is tender.

4 Remove the rice from the heat and stir in the ham, green bell pepper, red bell pepper, onion, parsley (if using), oil, lemon juice and lemon zest (if using).

5 Serve warm, at room temperature or chilled.

Step 2

TIME-SAVERS

■ **Do-ahead:** *The shrimp, ham and vegetables can be prepared ahead. The whole dish can be made ahead and served at room temperature or chilled.*

Values are approximate per serving: Calories: 423 Protein: 25 gm Fat: 16 gm
Carbohydrates: 45 gm Cholesterol: 121 mg Sodium: 976 mg

Step 4

Broiled Salmon with Lemon Mayonnaise

▼

Mayonnaise is a close relative of Hollandaise sauce, so it's not surprising that it makes a delectable topping for salmon fillets. In this recipe, lemon-flavored mayonnaise is spread over the fish before it is broiled, keeping the salmon succulent. For a tasty variation, substitute dill or tarragon for the parsley in the lemon mayonnaise. Serve the broiled fish with roasted new potatoes and a green vegetable.

Working time: 10 minutes
Total time: 20 minutes

Broiled Salmon with Lemon Mayonnaise

4 Servings

1 lemon
½ cup mayonnaise
2 tablespoons chopped parsley
(optional)

¼ teaspoon salt
¼ teaspoon pepper
4 salmon fillets (about 1¼ pounds total)

1 Preheat the broiler. Line a broiler pan with foil and lightly grease the foil.

2 Grate the lemon to make 1 tablespoon zest. Squeeze the lemon to make 2 tablespoons of juice.

3 In a small bowl, combine the mayonnaise, lemon juice, lemon zest, parsley (if using), salt and pepper.

4 Place the salmon fillets skin-side down on the prepared broiler pan. Spread them with half of the mayonnaise mixture.

5 Broil the fish 4 inches from the heat until the topping is golden, about 8 minutes. Serve the salmon with the remaining mayonnaise on the side.

TIME-SAVERS

■ **Do-ahead:** *The lemon mayonnaise (Step 3) can be made ahead.*

Values are approximate per serving: Calories: 402 Protein: 28 gm Fat: 31 gm
Carbohydrates: 2 gm Cholesterol: 94 mg Sodium: 354 mg

Step 2

Step 3

Step 4

Sesame Fish with Sweet-and-Sour Sauce

▼

In this recipe, delicate sesame-crusted fish fillet strips are accompanied by a warm, gingery sweet-and-sour fruit sauce. Although the sauce has a thoroughly Asian flavor, it is put together with American pantry staples—including pineapple juice, cider vinegar and ketchup—rather than exotic gourmet ingredients. Serve the fish with a Chinese-inspired salad of bamboo shoots and bok choy.

Working time: 20 minutes
Total time: 30 minutes

Sesame Fish with Sweet-and-Sour Sauce

4 Servings

3 cloves garlic
6 quarter-size slices (¼ inch thick) fresh ginger, unpeeled
4 scallions
4 tablespoons cornstarch
1 cup pineapple juice
½ cup plus 2 teaspoons vegetable oil
¼ cup cider vinegar

4 teaspoons reduced-sodium soy sauce
¼ cup ketchup
4 teaspoons sugar
½ teaspoon pepper
1 egg white
1¾ pounds halibut steaks, or other very firm white fish
½ cup sesame seeds

Step 3

1 In a food processor, mince the garlic. Add the ginger and coarsely chop. Add the scallions and coarsely chop. In a small bowl, combine 3 tablespoons of the cornstarch with the pineapple juice.

2 In a small skillet or saucepan, warm 2 teaspoons of the oil over medium-high heat until hot but not smoking. Add the garlic, ginger and scallions, and cook, stirring, until the garlic begins to brown, about 3 minutes.

3 Add the cornstarch-pineapple juice mixture, the vinegar, 2 teaspoons of the soy sauce, the ketchup, sugar and pepper, and bring to a boil over medium-high heat. Reduce the heat to low, cover and simmer while you prepare the fish.

4 In a shallow bowl, beat the egg white with the remaining 1 tablespoon cornstarch and 2 teaspoons soy sauce.

5 Cut the fish into ½-inch-wide strips. Add the fish to the egg white mixture and toss to coat well. Place the fish strips on a plate and sprinkle them with the sesame seeds, turning the fish to coat all sides.

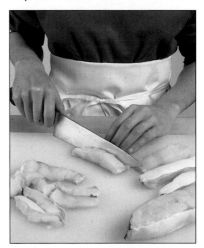

Step 5

6 In a medium nonstick skillet, warm the remaining ½ cup oil over medium-high heat until hot but not smoking. Add the fish in batches and cook until golden, about 3 minutes per side. As they are done, place the fish on a paper towel-lined plate in a low oven to keep warm.

7 Serve the fish with the hot sweet-and-sour sauce on the side.

TIME-SAVERS

■ *Do-ahead: The fish can be cut up ahead, or completely cooked ahead and served at room temperature. The sweet-and-sour sauce (Steps 1 through 3) can be made ahead and reheated (add a bit of water if it is too thick).*

Values are approximate per serving: Calories: 589 Protein: 47 gm Fat: 31 gm
Carbohydrates: 31 gm Cholesterol: 64 mg Sodium: 506 mg

Step 6

Spicy Shrimp
on Zucchini Nests

▼

*Sautéed shredded green and yellow squash form tasty "nests" for portions
of stir-fried shrimp in a zesty broth. Sprinkling the squash with salt and letting
it drain in a colander for a few minutes (while you prepare the shrimp)
draws out the excess moisture so the vegetables don't become swamped in liquid
while they cook.*

Working time: 30 minutes
Total time: 30 minutes

Spicy Shrimp on Zucchini Nests

4 Servings

2 large zucchini, unpeeled
2 large yellow squash, unpeeled
1 teaspoon salt
1 pound medium shrimp
4 tablespoons butter
2 tablespoons olive or other vegetable oil
¼ teaspoon black pepper

3 cloves garlic, minced or crushed through a press
⅓ cup chicken broth
2 tablespoons fine unseasoned breadcrumbs
½ teaspoon red pepper flakes
¼ cup chopped parsley (optional)

Step 2

1 In a food processor with the shredding blade, shred the zucchini and yellow squash lengthwise.

2 Layer the shredded squash in a colander, sprinkling it with the salt as you put it in. Set the colander in the sink to drain while you prepare the shrimp.

3 Shell and devein the shrimp.

4 Rinse the squash and drain well.

5 In a large skillet, melt 2 tablespoons of the butter in 1 tablespoon of the oil over medium-high heat until hot but not smoking. Add the shredded squash and cook, stirring, until the vegetables are just limp, 2 to 3 minutes.

Step 3

6 Stir in the black pepper. Remove the squash to a bowl and cover loosely to keep warm.

7 In the same skillet, melt the remaining 2 tablespoons butter in the remaining 1 tablespoon oil over medium-high heat until hot but not smoking. Add the garlic and the shrimp and stir-fry until the shrimp are just beginning to turn pink, about 3 minutes.

8 Add the chicken broth, bring to a boil and cook, stirring, for 1 minute. Add the breadcrumbs, red pepper flakes and parsley (if using) and cook until the shrimp are cooked through, about 1 minute longer.

9 To serve, use a slotted spoon to transfer some of the squash to a dinner plate and top the squash "nest" with some of the shrimp.

TIME-SAVERS

■ **Do-ahead:** *The shrimp can be shelled and deveined ahead of time.*

Step 8

Values are approximate per serving: Calories: 315 Protein: 22 gm Fat: 21 gm
Carbohydrates: 12 gm Cholesterol: 171 mg Sodium: 914 mg

Bluefish with Apples and Onion

The distinctive, almost meaty, flavor of fresh bluefish is complemented here with a lemon-mustard basting mixture and sautéed slices of onion and apple. In addition to its taste rewards, bluefish is also good for your health: A substance contained in fatty fish (such as bluefish, salmon and mackerel) has been shown to reduce blood cholesterol. Nutrition experts recommend that Americans add more fish to their diets.

Working time: 25 minutes
Total time: 30 minutes

Bluefish with Apples and Onion

4 Servings

4 bluefish fillets (about 1½ pounds total)
1 medium onion
1 large Granny Smith apple, unpeeled
2 tablespoons butter
¼ cup lemon juice
2 tablespoons olive or other vegetable oil

2 tablespoons Dijon mustard
2 teaspoons grated lemon zest (optional)
2 teaspoons dill
¼ teaspoon sugar
¼ teaspoon pepper
¼ cup chicken broth
2 tablespoons sour cream

Step 4

1 Preheat the broiler. Line a broiler pan with foil and lightly grease the foil. Place the bluefish skin-side up on the foil-lined pan.

2 Cut the onion and apple into thin wedges.

3 In a medium skillet, warm the butter over medium-high heat until melted. Add the onion and cook until the onion begins to brown, about 5 minutes.

4 Add the apple to the skillet and sauté until the apple begins to soften, about 3 minutes.

5 In a small bowl, combine the lemon juice, oil, mustard, lemon zest (if using), dill, sugar and pepper.

6 Remove 2 tablespoons of the lemon-mustard mixture and brush the fish with it. Broil the fish 4 inches from the heat for 8 to 10 minutes, or until it just flakes when tested with a fork.

Step 6

7 Meanwhile, add the remaining lemon-mustard mixture and the chicken broth to the skillet. Bring the mixture to a boil over medium-high heat and cook uncovered for about 3 minutes to reduce slightly.

8 Stir in the sour cream and remove the sauce from the heat.

9 Serve the fish topped with the sauce.

TIME-SAVERS

■ *Do-ahead: The onion and apple can be sautéed ahead. The lemon-mustard mixture (Step 5) can be made ahead.*

Step 8

Values are approximate per serving: Calories: 386 Protein: 35 gm Fat: 22 gm
Carbohydrates: 11 gm Cholesterol: 119 mg Sodium: 456 mg

Shallow-Fried Fish Tempura with Two Sauces

To make a Japanese tempura, pieces of chicken, seafood or vegetables are dipped in batter and quickly deep-fried. The result is delicate fritters with a crisp, fluffy crust. Here, pieces of fish are cooked tempura-style and served with two sauces: a creamy tartar sauce and a hot and gingery soy mixture. The frying technique for this recipe is manageable and neat, since you use a small saucepan and just 1 cup of oil.

Working time: 30 minutes
Total time: 30 minutes

Shallow-Fried Fish Tempura with Two Sauces

4 Servings

3 tablespoons reduced-sodium or regular soy sauce
2 tablespoons cider vinegar
1½ teaspoons Oriental sesame oil
⅛ teaspoon red pepper flakes
½ teaspoon black pepper
2 quarter-size slices (¼ inch thick) fresh ginger, unpeeled
¼ cup mayonnaise
¼ cup plain yogurt

3 tablespoons pickle relish, drained
1 pound firm-fleshed white fish fillet, such as scrod
⅓ cup cornstarch
2 tablespoons flour
½ teaspoon baking powder
½ teaspoon salt
1 egg
2 tablespoons water
1 cup vegetable oil

Step 3

1 In a small bowl, combine the soy sauce, vinegar, sesame oil, red pepper flakes and ⅛ teaspoon of the black pepper. Mince the ginger and add it to the bowl. Set the ginger-soy sauce aside.

2 In another small bowl, combine the mayonnaise, yogurt, pickle relish and ⅛ teaspoon of the black pepper. Refrigerate the tartar sauce until serving time.

3 Cut the fish into 1½-inch chunks.

4 In a medium bowl, combine the cornstarch, flour, baking powder, salt and the remaining ¼ teaspoon black pepper. In a small bowl, beat the egg with the water. Stir the egg mixture into the dry ingredients and beat to blend.

5 In a small saucepan, warm the oil until hot but not smoking (375° on a deep-fat thermometer).

Step 6

6 Meanwhile, dip the fish in the batter. When the oil is hot, add the fish in batches, without crowding, and cook until golden brown, about 3 minutes, turning the fish over once or twice as it cooks. Remove the fish chunks with a slotted spoon and drain them on paper towels. Keep the fish warm in a low oven while you cook the remaining batches.

7 Serve the fish with the sauces on the side.

TIME-SAVERS

■ ***Do-ahead:*** *The ginger-soy (Step 1) and tartar (Step 2) sauces can be made and the fish cut up well ahead.*

Values are approximate per serving: Calories: 405 Protein: 24 gm Fat: 25 gm
Carbohydrates: 20 gm Cholesterol: 111 mg Sodium: 1025 mg

Step 6

Pan-Braised Salmon with Green Sauce

In this simple braised fish entrée, the components of the accompanying green sauce—spinach, garlic, scallions and dill—cook right along with the salmon. Then the braised vegetables are puréed with sour cream to create a creamy pesto-like sauce. The braising liquid that remains is a flavorful broth that can be frozen and used later for poaching or braising fish or shellfish, or as the base for a fish soup or chowder.

Working time: 15 minutes
Total time: 25 minutes

4 Servings

3 cups low-sodium or regular chicken broth

3 cloves garlic, peeled

3 scallions

2 cups (packed) fresh spinach leaves or ¼ cup frozen spinach, thawed

¼ cup (packed) fresh dill sprigs or 1½ teaspoons dried

3 tablespoons lemon juice

4 small salmon steaks (about 1¾ pounds total)

2 tablespoons butter

1 tablespoon Dijon mustard

1½ teaspoons grated lemon zest (optional)

¼ teaspoon salt

¼ teaspoon pepper

½ cup sour cream

Step 3

1 In a large skillet, bring the chicken broth and whole garlic cloves to a boil over medium-high heat.

2 Meanwhile, wash and trim the scallions, spinach and fresh dill.

3 Add the whole scallions, spinach, dill, lemon juice and salmon steaks to the boiling broth. Reduce the heat to low, cover and simmer until the salmon just flakes when tested with a fork, 5 to 7 minutes.

4 With a slotted spatula, carefully remove the salmon to a plate and cover loosely to keep warm.

Step 5

5 With a slotted spoon, remove the garlic, scallions, spinach and dill to a food processor (reserve the broth for another use, if desired). Purée the cooked vegetables in the food processor. Add the butter, mustard, lemon zest (if using), salt and pepper.

6 Add the sour cream to the sauce and process to blend.

7 Serve the steaks topped with some of the sauce.

TIME-SAVERS

■ ***Microwave tip:*** *In a shallow microwave-safe baking dish, layer the spinach, whole scallions, whole garlic, dill sprigs and lemon juice. Place the salmon on top, with the rounded portions of the fish steaks toward the rim of the dish. Pour in 1 cup of broth. Cover and cook at 100% for 8 minutes, rotating the dish once about halfway through. Rotate the dish again and cook at 100% for another 2 to 4 minutes, depending on the size of the steaks.*

■ ***Do-ahead:*** *The vegetables can be prepared ahead. The whole dish can be prepared ahead and served at room temperature.*

Values are approximate per serving: Calories: 421 Protein: 42 gm Fat: 25 gm
Carbohydrates: 5 gm Cholesterol: 137 mg Sodium: 441 mg

Step 6

Fish Curry with Spinach and Peanuts

This fish curry has enough flavor to stand on its own, but it's fun to serve it with a selection of Indian-style condiments. Offer bowls of peanuts, sliced scallions, toasted coconut and perhaps a raita—a cooling blend of yogurt, chopped or shredded cucumbers and red onions. As always when using curry powder; season to taste: Serious curry lovers should add an extra one to two tablespoons of the spice blend.

Working time: 20 minutes
Total time: 25 minutes

Fish Curry with Spinach and Peanuts

4 Servings

1 package (10 ounces) frozen chopped spinach, thawed
1 medium onion
½ cup (packed) cilantro sprigs (optional)
1 tablespoon butter
1 tablespoon olive or other vegetable oil
3 cloves garlic, minced or crushed through a press

3 tablespoons flour
2 tablespoons curry powder
1 cup chicken broth
¼ teaspoon black pepper
Pinch of cayenne pepper
1 pound firm-fleshed white fish fillets, such as scrod
¼ cup sour cream
⅓ cup unsalted dry-roasted peanuts

Step 3

1 Place the spinach on several layers of paper towel to absorb excess moisture. Coarsely chop the onion. Mince the cilantro (if using).

2 In a large skillet, warm the butter in the oil over medium-high heat until the butter is melted. Add the garlic and onion and cook, stirring, until the onion is just translucent, about 3 minutes.

3 Stir in the flour and curry powder, and cook, stirring, until the flour is no longer visible, about 30 seconds. Stir in the chicken broth, black pepper, cayenne and 2 tablespoons of the cilantro. Bring the mixture to a boil over medium-high heat, stirring constantly.

4 Meanwhile, cut the fish into 1-inch cubes. Squeeze the spinach as dry as possible.

5 Add the fish and spinach to the boiling curry mixture. Reduce the heat to low, cover and simmer until the fish just flakes when tested with a fork, about 5 minutes.

6 Gently stir in the sour cream, peanuts and remaining cilantro.

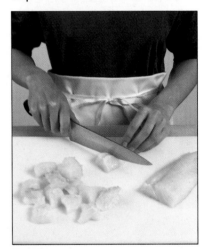
Step 4

TIME-SAVERS

■ *Do-ahead: The curry can be made ahead through Step 3. Gently reheat the curry mixture (adding a bit more chicken broth if it seems too thick) and proceed with Steps 4 through 6.*

Values are approximate per serving: Calories: 312   Protein: 28 gm   Fat: 17 gm
Carbohydrates: 14 gm   Cholesterol: 63 mg   Sodium: 400 mg

Step 6

Salmon Patties
with Citrus Vinaigrette

Enliven salmon patties with this tart-sweet sauce: a vinaigrette made
with fresh ginger, soy sauce, orange and lemon juice, and small pieces of
the fruits themselves. Ginger, cilantro and mustard mixed in
with the salmon give the tender fish cakes a unique flavor. Serve this
dish with a salad of Belgian endive, watercress and tomatoes.

Working time: 25 minutes
Total time: 30 minutes

Salmon Patties
with Citrus Vinaigrette

4 Servings

1 orange
1 lemon
3 scallions
6 quarter-size slices (¼ inch thick) fresh ginger, unpeeled
⅓ cup (packed) cilantro sprigs (optional)
¼ cup olive or other vegetable oil
2 teaspoons reduced-sodium soy sauce

2 drops hot pepper sauce
1 can (14¾ ounces) salmon, drained
1 cup fine unseasoned breadcrumbs
2 eggs
1 teaspoon dry mustard
¼ teaspoon pepper

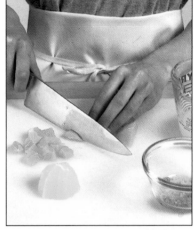

Step 1

1 Grate the orange to yield 2 teaspoons of zest. Grate the lemon to yield 2 teaspoons of zest. Halve the orange and lemon. Juice one orange half and one lemon half. Remove the peel and as much of the bitter white pith as possible from the unjuiced orange and lemon halves. Cut the peeled orange and lemon into bite-size pieces.

2 In a food processor, mince the scallions; remove and set aside. In the same processor work bowl, mince the ginger. Add the cilantro (if using) and finely chop.

3 In a small bowl, combine the orange and lemon zests, juices and pieces. Stir in 2 tablespoons of the oil, half of the ginger-cilantro mixture, the soy sauce and hot pepper sauce.

Step 4

4 In a medium bowl, combine the salmon, scallions and the remaining ginger-cilantro mixture, and toss to break up the salmon and distribute the ingredients.

5 Add the breadcrumbs, eggs, mustard and pepper, and thoroughly combine. Form the mixture into four patties about 4 inches in diameter.

6 In a large skillet, warm 1 tablespoon of the oil over medium-high heat until hot but not smoking. Add the salmon patties and cook until golden on one side, about 3 minutes. Turn the patties over, add the remaining 1 tablespoon oil and cook until golden on the second side, about 3 minutes. Serve the patties with the sauce on the side.

TIME-SAVERS

■ *Do-ahead: The citrus vinaigrette can be made and the salmon patties formed well ahead. The salmon patties can also be cooked a short time ahead and served at room temperature.*

Values are approximate per serving: Calories: 409 Protein: 26 gm Fat: 22 gm Carbohydrates: 26 gm Cholesterol: 141 mg Sodium: 741 mg

Step 5

Oriental Grilled Fish Salad

▼

Tuna salad has a well-deserved place in the American diet, but main-course fish salads have, in recent years, become more sophisticated. Here, cod (or halibut) steaks are grilled with a lime-ginger basting sauce, then served atop shredded Napa cabbage and red leaf lettuce. The remaining sauce is used to dress the salad. If necessary, substitute green cabbage for the Napa, but shred it very finely, as it is not as tender.

Working time: 20 minutes
Total time: 25 minutes

Oriental Grilled Fish Salad

4 Servings

4 quarter-size slices (¼ inch thick) fresh ginger, unpeeled
2 cloves garlic
¼ cup reduced-sodium soy sauce
3 tablespoons lime juice
2 tablespoons vegetable oil
1 tablespoon honey
1 teaspoon grated lime zest (optional)
¼ teaspoon black pepper
¼ teaspoon hot pepper flakes

1¼ pounds cod or halibut steaks
4 cups shredded Napa or Chinese cabbage (about 6 ounces)
4 cups shredded red leaf lettuce (about ½ head)
2 large carrots
2 cups bean sprouts (about ¼ pound)
2 tablespoons sesame seeds, toasted if desired

Step 3

1 Preheat the broiler or start the charcoal. If broiling, line a broiler pan with foil and lightly grease the foil.

2 In a food processor, finely chop the ginger and garlic. Add the soy sauce, lime juice, oil, honey, lime zest (if using), black pepper and hot pepper flakes and process to blend. Set aside half of the mixture to use as a salad dressing.

3 Place the fish on the grill or broiler pan and baste with half of the marinade. Grill or broil 4 inches from the heat for 5 minutes.

4 Meanwhile, shred the Napa cabbage and the lettuce. Cut the carrots into matchsticks.

Step 4

5 Turn the fish over and brush with the remaining marinade. Grill or broil until the fish just flakes when tested with a fork, about 5 minutes.

6 Meanwhile, divide the cabbage, lettuce, carrots and bean sprouts evenly among 4 dinner plates.

7 Cut the hot fish into ¾-inch chunks and place them on top of the greens. Pour the dressing over all. Sprinkle with the sesame seeds.

TIME-SAVERS

■ *Microwave tip: To toast sesame seeds, place them in a small microwave-safe bowl and toss with 1 teaspoon of oil. Cook at 100% until they begin to brown (they will continue to brown after you take them out of the oven), 4 to 6 minutes, stirring once or twice.*

■ *Do-ahead: The dressing-basting mixture (Step 2) can be made ahead. The fish can also be cooked ahead and the salad served at room temperature.*

Values are approximate per serving: Calories: 281 Protein: 30 gm Fat: 11 gm
Carbohydrates: 19 gm Cholesterol: 61 mg Sodium: 708 mg

Step 7

Parmesan Scallop Gratin

▼

This gratin is made with just a few ingredients and takes only 20 minutes to prepare, but you'd never suspect its simplicity when you taste it: Plump sea scallops in a creamy sauce are topped with a golden Parmesan-crumb crust. This is a perfect choice for a weeknight company meal, when time is short but you want to serve something special. Accompany the gratin with a green vegetable and uncork a dry white wine.

Working time: 15 minutes
Total time: 20 minutes

Parmesan Scallop Gratin

4 Servings

1 cup chicken broth
¼ teaspoon nutmeg
¼ teaspoon pepper, preferably white
1 pound sea scallops
2 tablespoons butter
1 tablespoon flour

¼ cup heavy cream
2 tablespoons grated Parmesan cheese
1 tablespoon fine, seasoned breadcrumbs
2 tablespoons chopped parsley (optional)

1 In a medium saucepan, bring the chicken broth, nutmeg and pepper to a boil over medium-high heat. Add the scallops and let the mixture return to a boil. Reduce the heat to low, cover and simmer until the scallops are barely cooked, about 3 minutes. With a slotted spoon, remove the scallops to a bowl and cover loosely to keep warm. Reserve the cooking liquid.

2 Preheat the broiler.

3 In a small saucepan, melt 1 tablespoon of the butter over medium heat until melted. Stir in the flour and cook, stirring, until the flour is no longer visible, about 15 seconds. Add the cream and ¼ cup of the reserved cooking liquid. Cook, stirring, until the mixture just starts to simmer and thicken, about 2 minutes. (If the sauce seems too thick, add a bit more cooking liquid.)

4 Combine the sauce and scallops, and toss to coat. Turn the mixture into a 1-quart gratin dish or shallow baking dish. Sprinkle with the Parmesan and breadcrumbs and dot with the remaining 1 tablespoon butter. Broil 4 inches from the heat until golden on top, 2 to 4 minutes. Garnish with the chopped parsley, if desired.

Values are approximate per serving: Calories: 238 Protein: 22 gm Fat: 13 gm
Carbohydrates: 6 gm Cholesterol: 76 mg Sodium: 600 mg

Step 1

Step 3

Step 4

Beer Batter Fillets
with Red Pepper Slaw

▼

*Batter-dipped fish has a thin, crackling-crisp crust that's not at all
greasy if the cooking oil is at the proper temperature; use a deep-fat thermometer
to determine this. It's best to fry in batches so the temperature of the
oil does not dip down too far. Keep the first batch of food warm in a low oven and
make sure the temperature of the oil is correct before you fry the second batch.*

Working time: 25 minutes
Total time: 25 minutes

Beer Batter Fillets
with Red Pepper Slaw

4 Servings

2 large red bell peppers	**⅔ cup flour**
1 small red onion	**2 tablespoons cornmeal**
3 tablespoons sour cream	**¾ teaspoon salt**
2 tablespoons lemon juice	**¼ teaspoon cayenne pepper**
2 teaspoons grated lemon zest (optional)	**1 egg**
	⅔ cup beer, preferably dark
½ teaspoon salt	**1½ cups vegetable oil**
¼ teaspoon black pepper	**4 small flounder or sole fillets**
Pinch of sugar	**(about 1½ pounds total)**
¼ cup chopped parsley (optional)	

Step 2

1 Thinly slice the bell peppers and the onion.

2 In a medium bowl, combine the sour cream, lemon juice, lemon zest (if using), salt, black pepper and sugar. Add the bell peppers, onion and parsley (if using). Toss to coat the ingredients well with the dressing.

3 In a shallow bowl, combine the flour, cornmeal, salt and cayenne. In a small bowl, lightly beat the egg. Stir the beer and beaten egg into the dry ingredients.

4 In a 10-inch skillet, heat the oil over medium heat until very hot but not smoking (about 375° on a deep-fat thermometer).

5 Dip the flounder into the batter and add it to the hot oil. Fry until golden brown, about 4 minutes; carefully turn the fish over halfway through. Drain the cooked fish on a paper towel-lined plate.

Step 5

6 Serve the fish with the red pepper slaw on the side.

TIME-SAVERS

■ *Do-ahead: The red pepper slaw can be made ahead.*

Values are approximate per serving: Calories: 444 Protein: 37 gm Fat: 20 gm
Carbohydrates: 26 gm Cholesterol: 140 mg Sodium: 851 mg

Step 5

Chicken Cucumber Salad with Tarragon (page 289)

CHAPTER 5
EXTRA-LIGHT

Italian Vegetable Enchiladas

Enchiladas—filled tortillas baked in a sauce—are Mexican in origin, but the filling and tomato sauce in this recipe have an Italian accent. The flour tortillas are wrapped around a mixture of cooked vegetables and cottage cheese; both the cheese and the sauce are flavored with quintessentially Italian basil and oregano. A topping of shredded mozzarella adds a final Italian touch.

Working time: 20 minutes
Total time: 30 minutes

Italian Vegetable Enchiladas

4 Servings

1 clove garlic
1 small onion
1 medium green bell pepper
½ pound mushrooms
1 medium tomato
1 tablespoon vegetable oil
1 can (8 ounces) low-sodium or regular tomato sauce

½ teaspoon basil
½ teaspoon oregano
½ teaspoon black pepper
1 cup low-fat cottage cheese
8 flour tortillas (7-inch diameter)
3 tablespoons shredded part-skim mozzarella cheese

1 Preheat the oven to 450°.

2 In a food processor, coarsely chop the garlic, onion and bell pepper. Remove to a large bowl. In the same work bowl, chop the mushrooms. Add to the other vegetables. By hand, coarsely chop the tomato and add to the bowl of vegetables.

3 In a large nonstick skillet, warm the oil over medium-high heat until hot but not smoking. Add the chopped vegetables and cook, stirring occasionally, until the onion is slightly softened, about 3 minutes. Let cool slightly.

4 Meanwhile, in a medium bowl, combine the tomato sauce, ¼ teaspoon of the basil, ¼ teaspoon of the oregano and ¼ teaspoon of the black pepper.

5 In another bowl, combine the cottage cheese with the remaining ¼ teaspoon basil, ¼ teaspoon oregano and ¼ teaspoon black pepper.

6 Place the tortillas on the work surface and spread each evenly with 2 teaspoons of the tomato sauce.

7 Spread 2 tablespoons of cottage cheese in a strip along the bottom third of each tortilla.

8 Dividing evenly, spread the sautéed vegetable mixture over the cottage cheese. Starting at the filled end, roll the tortillas up. Place the rolled tortillas in a single layer in a baking dish. Top with the remaining tomato sauce and the mozzarella.

9 Bake for 10 minutes, or until the tortillas are heated through and the cheese is melted. If desired, run the enchiladas under the broiler to lightly brown them.

Values are approximate per serving: Calories: 363 Protein: 17 gm Fat: 6 gm
Carbohydrates: 60 gm Cholesterol: 5 mg Sodium: 690 mg

Step 6

Step 7

Step 8

Spinach Fettuccine with Vegetable Ribbons

For this attractive dish, long "ribbons" of carrot and zucchini are tossed
with green fettuccine. For an even more colorful dish, use a half-and-half mixture
of spinach and regular pasta, or a combination of red (tomato), white, and green
fettuccine. A surprisingly rich and velvety—but low-calorie—sauce is made by using
cornstarch to thicken the broth in which the vegetable ribbons quickly cook.

Working time: 15 minutes
Total time: 25 minutes

Spinach Fettuccine with Vegetable Ribbons

4 Servings

2 medium carrots
2 medium zucchini, unpeeled
4 scallions
½ pound spinach fettuccine
1 cup low-sodium or regular chicken broth

2 cloves garlic, minced or crushed through a press
1 teaspoon oregano
¼ teaspoon pepper
2 tablespoons cornstarch
¼ cup grated Parmesan cheese

1 Bring a large pot of water to a boil.

2 Meanwhile, using a cheese slicer or a vegetable peeler, make long ribbons of carrot and zucchini. Coarsely chop the scallions.

3 Add the fettuccine to the boiling water and cook until al dente, 8 to 10 minutes, or according to package directions.

4 Meanwhile, in a large skillet, combine ¾ cup of the broth with the garlic, oregano and pepper, and bring to a boil. Add the carrot and zucchini ribbons, reduce the heat to medium-low, cover and simmer until the vegetables are wilted and tender, about 3 minutes.

5 With a slotted spoon, remove the carrot and zucchini to a serving bowl. Reserve the broth in the skillet. Drain the pasta and add it to the vegetable ribbons. Cover loosely to keep warm.

6 In a small bowl, combine the cornstarch and remaining ¼ cup broth and stir to blend. Bring the broth in the skillet to a boil over medium-high heat, stir in the cornstarch mixture and the scallions and cook, stirring, until the sauce has thickened slightly, about 1 minute.

7 Add the sauce and Parmesan to the pasta and vegetables and toss to coat.

TIME-SAVERS

■ *Do-ahead: The vegetables can be cut up a short time ahead.*

Step 2

Step 4

Step 6

Values are approximate per serving: Calories: 297   Protein: 13 gm   Fat: 5 gm
Carbohydrates: 52 gm   Cholesterol: 58 mg   Sodium: 164 mg

Light Mushroom and Pepper Frittata

The Italian frittata—basically a hearty omelet—is a wonderfully versatile dish. Cheese, chicken, seafood or just about any vegetable can be added to it. But unlike an omelet, a frittata requires no tricky technique and, best of all, it can be low in calories, fat and cholesterol: In this recipe, three eggs plus two egg whites stand in for the six to eight whole eggs used in a standard recipe.

Working time: 20 minutes
Total time: 30 minutes

Light Mushroom and Pepper Frittata

4 Servings

1 large red bell pepper	**3 whole eggs plus 2 egg whites**
1 bunch scallions (6 to 8)	**¼ teaspoon salt**
½ pound small mushrooms	**¼ teaspoon black pepper**
¼ cup chicken broth	**1 tablespoon margarine**
1 teaspoon thyme	

1 Cut the bell pepper into thin strips. Coarsely chop the scallions. Halve (or quarter) the mushrooms.

2 In a medium saucepan, bring the broth and ½ teaspoon of the thyme to a boil over medium-high heat. Add the bell pepper, scallions and mushrooms. Reduce the heat to medium-low, cover and simmer, stirring occasionally, until the bell pepper is crisp-tender, about 5 minutes.

3 Uncover the vegetables, increase the heat to medium and boil off any liquid remaining in the saucepan, 3 to 5 minutes.

4 Meanwhile, in a bowl, beat the whole eggs and egg whites together with the remaining ½ teaspoon thyme, the salt and black pepper.

5 Preheat the broiler.

6 Meanwhile, in a medium ovenproof skillet, melt the margarine over medium-high heat until hot but not smoking. Add the vegetables and the egg mixture and spread evenly in the pan. Reduce the heat to medium, cover and cook until almost set, 7 to 10 minutes.

7 When the frittata is almost set, place it under the broiler for about 5 minutes to complete the cooking and brown the top.

8 To serve, cut the frittata into pie-shaped wedges.

TIME-SAVERS

■ ***Do-ahead:*** *The vegetables can be cooked ahead through Step 3. The whole frittata can be made ahead and served at room temperature.*

Values are approximate per serving: Calories: 120 Protein: 9 gm Fat: 7 gm
Carbohydrates: 6 gm Cholesterol: 159 mg Sodium: 309 mg

Step 3

Step 6

Step 8

Fettuccine and Carrots
with Lemon-Dill Sauce

▼

*Cottage cheese has a lot to offer when it comes to low-calorie cooking. With
minor recipe alterations, it can often stand in for cream cheese, heavy cream or
sour cream. For this dish, standard (4% fat) cottage cheese works well, but
if you would prefer to use a lower-fat product, choose one that is dense and dry
rather than watery—pot-style cottage cheese, for example.*

Working time: 15 minutes
Total time: 20 minutes

Fettuccine and Carrots with Lemon-Dill Sauce

4 Servings

1 cup cottage cheese
¼ cup plain yogurt
⅓ cup shredded mozzarella cheese
2 tablespoons grated Parmesan cheese
1½ teaspoons grated lemon zest (optional)
3 medium carrots
½ cup low-sodium or regular chicken broth

3 tablespoons lemon juice
¼ teaspoon pepper, preferably white
3 scallions
⅓ cup chopped fresh dill or 1½ teaspoons dried
½ pound fettuccine

Step 2

1 Bring a large pot of water to a boil.

2 Meanwhile, in a food processor, purée the cottage cheese and yogurt until smooth. Add the mozzarella, Parmesan and lemon zest (if using), and process to blend.

3 Thinly slice the carrots.

4 In a medium saucepan, combine the chicken broth, 1 tablespoon of the lemon juice and the pepper. Cover and bring to a boil over medium-high heat. Add the carrots, reduce the heat to low, cover and simmer until the carrots are crisp-tender, about 5 minutes.

5 Meanwhile, coarsely chop the scallions and dill, then add to the carrots and broth and continue simmering while the pasta cooks.

Step 3

6 Add the pasta to the boiling water and cook until al dente, about 7 minutes, or according to package directions.

7 Drain the pasta and place it in a serving bowl. Add the broth and carrots, the remaining 2 tablespoons lemon juice and the cottage cheese mixture. Toss to blend the ingredients.

TIME-SAVERS

■ *Do-ahead:* *The cottage cheese mixture (Step 2) can be made ahead. The broth and carrots can be prepared ahead through Step 5, but should be brought back to a boil before tossing with the pasta.*

Step 7

Values are approximate per serving: Calories: 352   Protein: 19 gm   Fat: 8 gm   Carbohydrates: 51 gm   Cholesterol: 72 mg   Sodium: 346 mg

Chicken Breasts with Raisin-Wine Sauce

These lightly sauced chicken breasts are simple enough for an everyday meal, but pretty enough for company—and they're ready in less than half an hour. Steamed green beans are a good side dish for the chicken; for the salad course, try a mix of tart-flavored greens such as watercress or arugula. And since the chicken is low in calories, you might even splurge on dessert.

Working time: 15 minutes
Total time: 25 minutes

Chicken Breasts
with Raisin-Wine Sauce

4 Servings

3 quarter-size slices (¼ inch thick) fresh ginger, unpeeled
1 clove garlic
1 small onion
½ cup white grape juice or apple juice
¼ cup dry white wine
2 tablespoons apricot jam
½ teaspoon cinnamon
½ teaspoon salt
¼ teaspoon pepper
4 skinless, boneless chicken breast halves (about 1¼ pounds total)
¼ cup low-sodium chicken broth
2 tablespoons cornstarch
½ cup golden raisins

Step 3

1 Preheat the broiler. Line a broiler pan with foil.

2 In a food processor, mince the ginger and garlic. Add the onion and pulse on and off to finely chop.

3 In a small bowl, combine the ginger-onion mixture, the grape juice, wine, apricot jam, cinnamon, salt and pepper. Measure out ¼ cup of the mixture to use as a basting sauce for the chicken.

4 Place the chicken on the prepared broiler pan and brush with half of the basting sauce. Broil 4 inches from the heat for 4 minutes. Turn the chicken over, brush with the remaining basting sauce and broil for 4 minutes longer, or until the chicken is cooked through.

Step 4

5 Meanwhile, in a small bowl, blend the chicken broth and the cornstarch. In a medium skillet, bring the remaining grape juice mixture to a boil over medium-high heat, and then stir in the cornstarch mixture. Add the raisins and cook, stirring, until the sauce thickens slightly, about 2 minutes.

6 Add the cooked chicken to the skillet (along with any juices from the broiler pan) and cook until heated through, 1 to 2 minutes.

7 Serve the chicken topped with some of the sauce.

TIME-SAVERS

■ **Do-ahead:** *The grape juice mixture (Steps 2 and 3) can be made and the raisin sauce (Step 5) cooked ahead.*

Step 6

Values are approximate per serving: Calories: 292 Protein: 34 gm Fat: 2 gm
Carbohydrates: 32 gm Cholesterol: 82 mg Sodium: 377 mg

Turkey Stir-Fry
with Corn and Broccoli

Stir-fries make great light meals because they can include lots of vegetables
and modest amounts of meat. And the skinless turkey breast used here is lower in
fat and calories than any other type of poultry or meat. In this recipe the
rice is tossed with the stir-fry before serving, but you could also mound some
rice on each plate and spoon the vegetables and turkey on top.

Working time: 25 minutes
Total time: 30 minutes

Turkey Stir-Fry with Corn and Broccoli

4 Servings

2 cups low-sodium or regular
  chicken broth
¾ cup raw rice
2 stalks broccoli
1 medium red onion
3 turkey cutlets (about ½ pound
  total)
2 tablespoons flour
½ teaspoon salt
¼ teaspoon pepper

1 tablespoon olive or other
  vegetable oil
1 cup frozen corn, thawed
3 cloves garlic, minced or crushed
  through a press
3 tablespoons lemon juice
1 teaspoon grated lemon zest
  (optional)
¾ teaspoon thyme

Step 2

1 In a medium saucepan, bring 1¾ cups of the broth to a boil. Add the rice, reduce the heat to medium-low, cover and simmer until tender, 15 to 20 minutes.

2 Meanwhile, cut the broccoli into bite-size pieces. Thinly slice the onion. Cut the turkey cutlets into ¼-inch-wide strips.

3 In a shallow bowl, combine the flour, salt and pepper. Lightly dredge the turkey strips in the seasoned flour.

4 In a large nonstick skillet, warm the oil until hot but not smoking. Add the turkey strips and stir-fry over medium-high heat until cooked through, about 6 minutes. Remove the turkey to a plate and cover loosely to keep warm.

5 Add the remaining ¼ cup broth to the skillet over medium-high heat. Add the broccoli, onion, corn and garlic, and cook for 2 minutes.

Step 5

6 Add the lemon juice, lemon zest (if using) and thyme and bring to a boil. Reduce the heat to medium-low, cover and simmer until the vegetables are just tender, about 5 minutes.

7 Return the turkey to the skillet, add the cooked rice and toss well to combine.

TIME-SAVERS

■ *Do-ahead: The turkey and vegetables can all be cut up ahead. The rice can be cooked ahead and reheated very briefly in the microwave before tossing with the stir-fry.*

Values are approximate per serving: Calories: 316 Protein: 21 gm Fat: 6 gm
Carbohydrates: 46 gm Cholesterol: 35 mg Sodium: 360 mg

Step 7

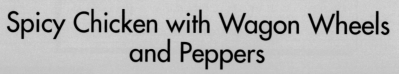

Spicy Chicken with Wagon Wheels and Peppers

▼

Not long ago, the idea of a low-calorie dish made with pasta and potatoes would have seemed laughable. Today, we know that the complex carbohydrates found in grains and vegetables are the best basis for any healthy diet; it's what you add to them that can make them high in fat and calories. This hearty dish is prepared with skinless chicken breast, less than an ounce of Parmesan, and no oil or butter.

Working time: 20 minutes
Total time: 30 minutes

Spicy Chicken with Wagon Wheels and Peppers

6 Servings

3 cups low-sodium or regular chicken broth
1 cup water
2 cloves garlic, minced or crushed through a press
3 drops hot pepper sauce
¼ to ½ teaspoon red pepper flakes, to taste
¼ teaspoon black pepper

2 large or 3 medium sweet potatoes (about 1 pound)
½ pound wagon wheel pasta (about 4 cups)
1 large green bell pepper
½ pound skinless, boneless chicken breast
3 tablespoons grated Parmesan cheese

Step 2

1 In a large skillet, combine the chicken broth, water, garlic, hot pepper sauce, red pepper flakes and black pepper, and bring to a boil over medium-high heat.

2 Meanwhile, peel the sweet potatoes and cut into ¼-inch dice.

3 When the broth has come to a boil, add the sweet potatoes and pasta. Stir and return the liquid to a boil. Reduce the heat to medium-low, cover and simmer until the pasta is al dente, about 7 minutes.

4 Meanwhile, cut the bell pepper into thin strips. Cut the chicken across the grain into ¼-inch-wide strips.

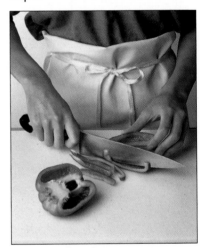

Step 4

5 Return the mixture in the skillet to a boil over medium-high heat. Stir in the bell pepper and chicken. Let the mixture return to a boil, then reduce the heat to medium-low, cover and simmer, stirring occasionally, until the chicken is cooked through, 5 to 7 minutes.

6 Stir in the Parmesan and serve.

TIME-SAVERS

■ **Do-ahead:** *The vegetables and chicken can be cut up ahead.*

Step 5

Values are approximate per serving: Calories: 272 Protein: 17 gm Fat: 3 gm
Carbohydrates: 44 gm Cholesterol: 24 mg Sodium: 110 mg

Herbed Turkey Burgers

▼

Big, juicy and every bit as satisfying as beef burgers, these ground turkey patties are low in fat and calories. This recipe calls for unseasoned bread crumbs, which you can easily make yourself: just process stale sliced bread in a food processor or blender. It will take about two slices of bread to make the amount of breadcrumbs called for here, but you can process several cups of crumbs and store them in the freezer.

Working time: 20 minutes
Total time: 20 minutes

Herbed Turkey Burgers

4 Servings

1 small onion	2 teaspoons Worcestershire sauce
2 cloves garlic	1 egg white
¼ cup (packed) parsley sprigs	1 teaspoon oregano
1 pound ground turkey	¼ teaspoon pepper
½ cup fine unseasoned breadcrumbs	1 teaspoon olive or other vegetable oil
2 tablespoons Dijon mustard	

1 In a food procesor, mince the onion, garlic and parsley.

2 In a medium bowl, combine the minced vegetables with the turkey, breadcrumbs, mustard, Worcestershire sauce, egg white, oregano and pepper, and mix to blend well.

3 Divide the mixture into 4 equal portions and form them into patties ½ inch thick.

4 In a large nonstick skillet, warm the oil over medium-high heat until hot but not smoking. Add the turkey patties and cook until well browned on both sides, 3 to 5 minutes for the first side and 2 to 4 minutes for the second side.

TIME-SAVERS

■ **Do-ahead:** *The turkey patties can be formed ahead and refrigerated or frozen.*

Values are approximate per serving: Calories: 267 Protein: 23 gm Fat: 14 gm Carbohydrates: 13 gm Cholesterol: 77 mg Sodium: 466 mg

Step 1

Step 2

Step 3

Veal Patties in Parsley Cream Sauce

Cream sauces are not usually low-calorie fare. But it is possible to whip up a creamy low-fat sauce using chicken broth, evaporated skimmed milk, a bit of flour and the pan juices from the veal patties. The sauce is thick and smooth, as velvety as if you'd used heavy cream. Dipping the veal patties in egg white rather than whole eggs helps to reduce the fat and cholesterol content of the dish also.

Working time: 20 minutes
Total time: 25 minutes

Veal Patties in Parsley Cream Sauce

4 Servings

1 medium onion	**½ teaspoon nutmeg**
⅓ cup (packed) parsley sprigs	**¼ teaspoon allspice**
1 egg white	**¼ teaspoon pepper**
½ pound ground veal	**1 tablespoon olive oil**
⅔ cup fine unseasoned	**1 tablespoon flour**
breadcrumbs	**1 cup low-sodium chicken broth**
¾ cup evaporated skimmed milk	

Step 2

1 Finely chop the onion. Mince the parsley.

2 In a medium bowl, beat the egg white until frothy. Stir in the onion, half of the parsley, the veal, breadcrumbs, ¼ cup of the evaporated skimmed milk, the nutmeg, allspice and pepper. Form the mixture into 4 patties a scant ½ inch thick.

3 In a large nonstick skillet, warm the oil over medium-high heat until hot but not smoking. Add the patties and cook until browned, 3 to 4 minutes per side. Remove the patties to a plate and cover loosely to keep warm.

4 In a small bowl, combine the remaining ½ cup evaporated skimmed milk and the flour, and blend well.

Step 2

5 Add the chicken broth to the skillet and bring to a boil over medium-high heat, scraping up any browned bits from the bottom of the pan. Stir in the flour-milk mixture and cook, stirring, until the sauce has thickened slightly, about 2 minutes.

6 Stir the remaining parsley into the skillet. Return the veal patties (and any juices that have accumulated on the plate) to the skillet and cook to coat the patties with the sauce and heat through, 1 to 2 minutes.

TIME-SAVERS

■ **Do-ahead:** *The veal patties can be formed ahead.*

Step 6

Values are approximate per serving: Calories: 245 Protein: 19 gm Fat: 9 gm
Carbohydrates: 22 gm Cholesterol: 49 mg Sodium: 255 mg

Broiled Pork Chops
with Nectarine Chutney

The colorful and piquant fruit chutney that accompanies these juicy chops is made with nectarines, but it can also be prepared with peaches or pineapple. For a peach chutney, use one pound of fresh or frozen fruit (do not use canned peaches). Blanch the fresh peaches in boiling water for 1 minute, then peel them before chopping. For a pineapple chutney, drain a 20-ounce can of juice-packed pineapple chunks.

Working time: 20 minutes
Total time: 20 minutes

Broiled Pork Chops with Nectarine Chutney

4 Servings

1 pound nectarines
1 small onion
6 quarter-size slices (¼ inch thick) fresh ginger, unpeeled
1½ teaspoons grated lemon zest (optional)
2 tablespoons lemon juice
1 tablespoon orange juice concentrate

1 tablespoon cider vinegar
2 tablespoons brown sugar
1 tablespoon cinnamon
1 tablespoon olive or other vegetable oil
¼ teaspoon pepper
4 center-cut pork chops (¼ inch thick, about 1 pound total), well trimmed

1 Coarsely chop the nectarines and onion. Mince the ginger.

2 In a medium saucepan, combine the nectarines, onion, half the ginger, the lemon zest (if using), 1 tablespoon of the lemon juice, the orange juice concentrate, vinegar, brown sugar and 1½ teaspoons of the cinnamon. Bring to a boil over medium-high heat. Reduce the heat to low, cover and simmer while you broil the pork chops.

3 Preheat the broiler. Line a broiler pan with foil.

4 In a small bowl, combine the olive oil, the remaining 1 tablespoon lemon juice, remaining ginger, 1½ teaspoons cinnamon and the pepper.

5 Place the pork chops on the prepared broiling pan. Brush them with half the olive oil mixture, and broil 4 inches from the heat for 4 minutes.

6 Turn the pork chops over, brush them with the remaining olive oil mixture and broil for 4 minutes longer, or until cooked through.

7 Serve the chops with the nectarine chutney on the side.

TIME-SAVERS

■ ***Do-ahead:*** *The nectarine chutney (Steps 1 and 2) and the basting mixture (Step 4) can be made ahead.*

Values are approximate per serving: Calories: 249 Protein: 18 gm Fat: 10 gm
Carbohydrates: 24 gm Cholesterol: 52 mg Sodium: 46 mg

Step 1

Step 2

Step 5

Veal Scallopini with Minted Rice-Carrot Pilaf

▼

The veal in this Italian-style recipe is infused with the flavors of a Milanese specialty called "gremolata," a blend of chopped lemon zest, garlic and parsley. Usually served as an accompaniment to meat dishes such as "osso buco" (braised veal shanks), gremolata is sometimes made with half lemon and half orange zest—a variation you might try if you have an orange on hand.

Working time: 20 minutes
Total time: 30 minutes

Veal Scallopini with Minted Rice-Carrot Pilaf

4 Servings

2 medium carrots
2½ cups chicken broth
2 teaspoons grated lemon zest
1½ teaspoons mint
½ teaspoon pepper
1 cup raw rice
¼ cup fine unseasoned breadcrumbs
¾ teaspoon oregano

8 veal scallopini (about 1 pound total)
1 tablespoon olive or other vegetable oil
2 tablespoons lemon juice
1 teaspoon cornstarch
1 clove garlic, minced or crushed through a press
¼ cup chopped parsley

Step 2

1 In a food processor, shred the carrots.

2 In a medium saucepan, combine 2 cups of the chicken broth, 1 teaspoon of the lemon zest, the mint and ¼ teaspoon of the pepper. Add the carrots and rice and bring to a boil over medium-high heat. Reduce the heat to low, cover and simmer until the rice is tender and all the liquid is absorbed, 15 to 20 minutes.

3 Meanwhile, in a shallow bowl, combine the breadcrumbs, oregano and remaining ¼ teaspoon pepper. Lightly dredge the veal in the seasoned breadcrumbs.

4 In a large skillet, warm the oil over medium-high heat until hot but not smoking. Add the veal and sauté until golden on both sides, about 3 minutes total. Remove the veal to a plate and cover loosely to keep warm.

Step 4

5 In a small bowl, stir together the remaining ½ cup chicken broth, 1 teaspoon lemon zest, the lemon juice, cornstarch, garlic and 2 tablespoons of the parsley. Add this mixture to the skillet and stir to combine. Bring the mixture to a boil, return the veal (and any juices that have accumulated on the plate) to the skillet and cook until heated through, about 1 minute.

6 Top the veal with pan juices. Stir the remaining chopped parsley into the pilaf and serve alongside the veal.

TIME-SAVERS

■ *Do-ahead: The rice-carrot pilaf can be made ahead and quickly reheated in the microwave.*

Values are approximate per serving: Calories: 386 Protein: 31 gm Fat: 7 gm
Carbohydrates: 48 gm Cholesterol: 89 mg Sodium: 754 mg

Step 5

Zesty Tuna with Mexican Seasonings in Lettuce Cups

For this light entrée, tuna is treated like a taco filling and spooned into nests of lettuce instead of deep-fried tortillas. Boston, Bibb and buttercrunch lettuce leaves are the right shape for this—they naturally curl into a cup. The tuna-vegetable mixture is topped with oven-toasted tortilla strips (these low-salt, low-fat "chips" make good snacks, too). But if time is short, you could just use crumbled storebought tortilla chips.

Working time: 20 minutes
Total time: 25 minutes

Zesty Tuna with Mexican Seasonings in Lettuce Cups

4 Servings

4 corn tortillas
3 medium plum tomatoes
2 medium carrots
4 scallions
¼ cup cilantro sprigs (optional)
1 can (7 ounces) water-packed tuna, drained
3½ tablespoons lime juice
1 tablespoon olive or other vegetable oil
3 drops hot pepper sauce

1 clove garlic, minced or crushed through a press
1½ teaspoons grated lime zest (optional)
¾ teaspoon oregano
½ teaspoon cumin
½ teaspoon salt
¼ teaspoon pepper
8 Boston, Bibb or buttercrunch lettuce leaves
½ cup plain yogurt

Step 3

1 Preheat the oven to 375°.

2 Cut the tortillas into ¼-inch-wide strips. Place the strips on a baking sheet and bake for 10 minutes, or until crisp.

3 Meanwhile, coarsely chop the tomatoes, carrots, scallions and cilantro (if using).

4 Place the tuna in a large bowl and flake apart with a fork. Add the chopped vegetables and cilantro (if using), and toss together.

Step 4

5 In a small bowl, combine the lime juice, oil, hot pepper sauce, garlic, lime zest (if using), oregano, cumin, salt and pepper.

6 Pour the dressing over the tuna and vegetables and toss to distribute the dressing.

7 Place the lettuce leaves on a platter. Divide the tuna mixture among the lettuce leaves. Serve 2 lettuce cups per person and top each with tortilla strips and 1 tablespoon of yogurt.

TIME-SAVERS

■ **Do-ahead:** *The tortilla strips can be prepared ahead. The tuna mixture can be made ahead, but don't add the chopped tomatoes until just before serving or the mixture may get too watery.*

Step 7

Values are approximate per serving: Calories: 206   Protein: 18 gm   Fat: 5 gm
Carbohydrates: 23 gm   Cholesterol: 20 mg   Sodium: 525 mg

Unfried Rice
with Chicken and Carrots

Real Chinese fried rice is delicious, but since it is made with eggs, lots of soy sauce and, often, bits of meat, it is loaded with fat and sodium. This savory "unfried" version re-creates the flavor combinations with a lot less fat. The rice is cooked in broth for full flavor; chicken, scallions and carrots round out the dish; and an egg white (most of the calories and all of the fat are in the yolk) is added for an authentic texture.

Working time: 20 minutes
Total time: 30 minutes

Unfried Rice with Chicken and Carrots

6 Servings

3 quarter-size slices (¼ inch thick) fresh ginger, unpeeled
3 cloves garlic
2½ cups low-sodium or regular chicken broth
1 cup raw rice
2 tablespoons reduced-sodium soy sauce
1 tablespoon Oriental sesame oil
1 tablespoon rice vinegar

¼ teaspoon red pepper flakes
¼ teaspoon black pepper
4 scallions
¼ cup (packed) cilantro sprigs (optional)
2 medium carrots
¾ pound skinless, boneless chicken breast
1 egg white

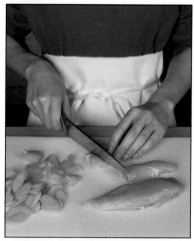

Step 4

1 In a food processor, finely chop the ginger and garlic.

2 In a medium saucepan, bring 2 cups of the chicken broth to a boil over medium-high heat. Add the rice, reduce the heat to medium-low, cover and simmer until the rice is tender and all the liquid is absorbed, about 20 minutes.

3 Meanwhile, in a medium skillet, bring the remaining ½ cup broth to a boil. Add the ginger-garlic mixture, the soy sauce, sesame oil, vinegar, red pepper flakes and black pepper. Reduce the heat to low, cover and simmer while you prepare the remaining ingredients.

4 In a food processor, finely chop the scallions and the cilantro (if using). Thinly slice the carrots. Cut the chicken into bite-size pieces.

Step 6

5 Return the broth to a boil over medium-high heat. Add the carrots and chicken. Let the broth return to a boil, then cover and cook until the chicken is cooked through, 1 to 2 minutes.

6 In a small bowl, beat the egg white. Stir the beaten egg white into the boiling broth. Then stir in the cooked rice, scallions and cilantro (if using), and serve.

TIME-SAVERS

■ *Do-ahead: The rice can be cooked ahead of time, or you can use leftover rice; fluff the grains slightly before stirring the rice into the seasoned broth (Step 6). The scallions, cilantro, carrots and chicken can be cut up ahead.*

Step 6

Values are approximate per serving: Calories: 230 Protein: 18 gm Fat: 4 gm
Carbohydrates: 30 gm Cholesterol: 33 mg Sodium: 279 mg

Broiled Fish Steaks with Tomato-Bell Pepper Relish

▼

This quick and flavorful relish of chopped tomatoes, red bell pepper, scallions and basil in a vinaigrette base performs double duty: The chunky relish serves as a condiment, while the vinaigrette is used to baste the fish before it is broiled. Although fresh tomatoes are best for this recipe, canned tomatoes can be used in a pinch.

Working time: 10 minutes
Total time: 15 minutes

Broiled Fish Steaks with Tomato-Bell Pepper Relish

4 Servings

4 medium plum tomatoes (about ¾ pound total) or 1 can (14 ounces) whole tomatoes, well drained
1 small red bell pepper
3 scallions
¼ cup fresh basil leaves or 1½ teaspoons dried

2 tablespoons olive or other vegetable oil
2 tablespoons red wine vinegar or cider vinegar
½ teaspoon black pepper
¼ teaspoon salt
4 tuna, cod or halibut steaks (¾ inch thick, about 1 pound total)

1 Preheat the broiler. Line a broiler pan with foil and lightly grease the foil.

2 Coarsely chop the tomatoes; set aside. In a food processor, coarsely chop the bell pepper, scallions and basil.

Step 2

3 Transfer the vegetable mixture to a bowl. Stir in the chopped tomatoes, the oil, vinegar, black pepper and salt, and stir until well mixed.

4 Place the fish steaks on the prepared broiler pan.

5 Strain the excess liquid from the tomato-bell pepper relish into a small bowl. Brush the fish with some of the liquid and broil 4 inches from the heat for 4 minutes. Turn the fish over and brush with some more of the liquid; broil until the fish just flakes when tested with a fork, about 4 minutes longer.

Step 3

6 Serve the fish steaks topped with the tomato-bell pepper relish.

TIME-SAVERS

■ **Microwave tip:** *Microwaving will produce a fish that is more poached than broiled, but this method will also keep the kitchen cooler if you are cooking in hot weather. Place the fish in a shallow microwave-safe baking dish. Brush the fish with the liquid from the tomato-bell pepper relish (see Step 5 above) and cover loosely with plastic wrap. Cook at 100% for 6 minutes, rotating the dish once. Let the dish stand, covered, for 3 minutes.*

■ **Do-ahead:** *The tomato-bell pepper relish can be made well ahead.*

Values are approximate per serving: Calories: 245 Protein: 27 gm Fat: 13 gm
Carbohydrates: 5 gm Cholesterol: 43 mg Sodium: 186 mg

Step 5

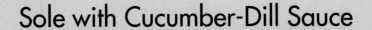

Sole with Cucumber-Dill Sauce

▼

A lighter, fresher-tasting twist on mayonnaise-based tartar sauce, the cucumber-dill sauce served with this broiled fish is made with dill, chopped cucumber, bell pepper and low-fat yogurt. A mainstay of the low-calorie kitchen, yogurt can stand in for mayonnaise or sour cream in many sauces and dressings. If you have some cucumber left over after making the sauce, slice it thin and use it as a garnish.

Working time: 15 minutes
Total time: 15 minutes

Sole with Cucumber-Dill Sauce

4 Servings

2-inch length of cucumber
¼ of a small red bell pepper (to make ¼ cup minced)
¼ cup packed fresh dill sprigs or 1½ teaspoons dried dill
1 tablespoon margarine
½ teaspoon salt
½ teaspoon black pepper

4 small sole fillets or other firm-fleshed white fish (about 1½ pounds total)
1 cup plain yogurt
3 tablespoons lemon juice
2 teaspoons grated lemon zest (optional)
½ teaspoon dry mustard

Step 2

1 Preheat the broiler. Line a broiler pan with foil and very lightly grease the foil.

2 Peel and finely chop the cucumber. Mince the bell pepper. Mince the fresh dill. Melt the margarine in a small saucepan or in the microwave.

3 In a small bowl, combine the melted margarine with 1 tablespoon of the fresh dill (or ½ teaspoon of the dried), ¼ teaspoon of the salt and ¼ teaspoon of the black pepper.

4 Place the fish on the prepared broiler pan. Spread the dill mixture over the fish and broil 4 inches from the heat until the fish is opaque and just flakes when tested with a fork, about 7 minutes.

5 Meanwhile, in a medium bowl, combine the yogurt, lemon juice, lemon zest (if using), mustard, the remaining 3 tablespoons fresh dill (or 1 teaspoon dried), ¼ teaspoon salt and ¼ teaspoon black pepper. Stir in the cucumber and bell pepper.

6 Serve the fish with the cucumber-dill sauce on the side.

Step 4

TIME-SAVERS

■ ***Microwave tip:*** *Although cooking the fish in the microwave will not save any time, it will keep the kitchen cooler in the summer, and the microwaved fish will be moister than the broiled version. Place the fish in a shallow microwave-safe baking dish and spread the dill mixture on them, as directed. Cover loosely with waxed paper and cook at 100% for 6 minutes, rotating the dish once.*

■ ***Do-ahead:*** *The cucumber-dill sauce (Step 5) can be made ahead, although it would be better to stir in the cucumber at the last moment to prevent the sauce from getting watery.*

Values are approximate per serving: Calories: 226   Protein: 35 gm   Fat: 6 gm
Carbohydrates: 6 gm   Cholesterol: 85 mg   Sodium: 488 mg

Step 5

Chicken-Cucumber Salad with Tarragon

Most storebought chicken salads are a dieter's disaster—small shreds of chicken floating in a sea of mayonnaise. This warm homemade salad, however, boasts good-sized pieces of chicken, cucumber and bell pepper, tossed with a light, tarragon-flavored yogurt dressing. Pack any leftover salad for the next day's lunch: Line a leakproof container with lettuce before packing the salad.

Working time: 15 minutes
Total time: 25 minutes

Chicken-Cucumber Salad
with Tarragon

4 Servings

2 skinless, boneless chicken breast halves (about ¾ pound total)
¼ cup (loosely packed) fresh tarragon or 1½ teaspoons dried
½ cup chicken broth
2 cloves garlic, minced or crushed through a press
¼ teaspoon black pepper
1 medium cucumber

1 large red bell pepper
1 tablespoon olive or other vegetable oil
1 tablespoon rice wine vinegar or white wine vinegar
⅓ cup plain yogurt
½ teaspoon salt
8 Boston lettuce leaves

Step 1

1 Cut the chicken breasts across the grain into thin slices. Mince the tarragon.

2 In a medium saucepan, bring the chicken broth, half of the tarragon, the garlic and black pepper to a boil over medium-high heat. Add the chicken slices and return to a boil. Reduce the heat to low, cover and simmer, stirring occasionally, until the chicken is cooked through, about 7 minutes.

3 Meanwhile, peel the cucumber and cut into small cubes. Coarsely chop the bell pepper.

4 In a small bowl, combine the oil, vinegar, yogurt, salt and remaining tarragon.

5 Transfer the chicken to a serving bowl (discard the broth or reserve for another use). Add the cucumber, bell pepper and yogurt dressing, and toss to combine.

6 Line individual serving plates with 2 lettuce leaves and spoon the salad on top.

Step 3

TIME-SAVERS

■ *Microwave tip: To cook the chicken, combine only ¼ cup of chicken broth with half the tarragon, the garlic, pepper and chicken in a microwave-safe casserole. Cover loosely and cook at 100% for 5 minutes, or until the chicken is cooked through, stirring once.*

■ *Do-ahead: The chicken can be cooked or the whole salad assembled ahead of time.*

Values are approximate per serving: Calories: 158 Protein: 22 gm Fat: 5 gm
Carbohydrates: 6 gm Cholesterol: 50 mg Sodium: 379 mg

Step 6

Tuna-Spinach Salad with Peanut Dressing

▼

The orange juice in this low-fat salad dressing requires somewhat less oil to mellow it than do more acidic ingredients such as vinegar or lemon juice. Peanut butter, which contains about one-third less fat than oil, gives the dressing a nutty taste, which is reinforced by a single tablespoon of Oriental sesame oil. If you can find them, try radish or alfalfa sprouts in place of the bean sprouts.

Working time: 25 minutes
Total time: 25 minutes

6 Servings

2 navel oranges
2 tablespoons smooth peanut butter
2 tablespoons reduced-sodium soy sauce
2 teaspoons ground ginger
2 tablespoons cider vinegar
1 tablespoon Oriental sesame oil
¼ teaspoon pepper
8 cups (loosely packed) fresh spinach leaves (about 6 ounces)

¼ pound mushrooms
2 medium carrots
1 small red onion
1½ cups bean sprouts (about ¼ pound)
2 cans (6½ ounces each) water-packed tuna, drained
¼ cup (packed) cilantro sprigs (optional)

Step 2

1 Grate the zest from the oranges. Juice the oranges and measure out ⅔ cup.

2 In a small bowl, blend the peanut butter, soy sauce and ground ginger. Stir in the orange juice and zest, the vinegar, sesame oil and pepper.

3 Tear the spinach into bite-size pieces. Slice the mushrooms. Cut the carrots into thin slices or matchsticks. Thinly slice the onion.

4 Mound the prepared vegetables on 4 individual salad plates or a single serving platter. Top with the bean sprouts and flaked tuna.

5 Coarsely chop the cilantro (if using) and stir it into the dressing. Spoon the dressing over the salad.

Step 3

TIME-SAVERS

■ *Do-ahead: The dressing can be made ahead. The spinach, carrots and onion can be prepared ahead.*

Values are approximate per serving: Calories: 174 Protein: 20 gm Fat: 6 gm
Carbohydrates: 11 gm Cholesterol: 23 mg Sodium: 454 mg

Step 4

Summer Fruit Salad with Fresh Strawberry-Yogurt Dressing

▼

If you buy a fresh pineapple for this fruit salad, don't try to judge it by its apparent ripeness. Since pineapples do not continue to ripen after they've been picked (they'll get softer and juicier, but not sweeter), your best bet is to look for a label indicating that the fruit was jet-shipped from Hawaii: These pineapples are most likely to be in prime condition.

Working time: 25 minutes
Total time: 25 minutes

Summer Fruit Salad with Fresh Strawberry-Yogurt Dressing

6 Servings

1 large pineapple or 4 cups canned pineapple chunks	**2 limes**
1 cup blueberries	**1 cup plain yogurt**
Half a medium cantaloupe	**2 tablespoons honey**
1 pint strawberries	**½ teaspoon vanilla extract**

Step 1

1 Halve the pineapple lengthwise, leaving the leaves on and cutting through the crown. Using a grapefruit knife (or other sharp flexible knife), loosen the fruit from the skin of the pineapple, leaving a ½-inch-thick shell; set the pineapple shells aside. Cut the cores out of the pineapple flesh and cut the fruit into bite-size pieces. Place the fruit in a medium bowl. Add the blueberries to the bowl.

2 With a melon baller (or teaspoon) scoop the flesh out of the cantaloupe half. Add the cantaloupe to the bowl of fruit. Halve the strawberries and place half of them in the bowl with the other fruit. Set the remaining strawberries aside.

3 Grate the zest from the limes and then juice them. Add the lime juice and zest to the bowl of fruit and toss to combine. Dividing evenly, scoop the fruit into the pineapple shells.

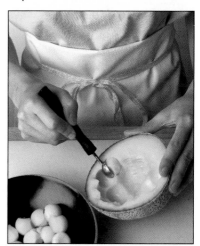

Step 2

4 In a small bowl, mash the remaining strawberries with a fork. Stir in the yogurt, honey and vanilla. Serve the dressing on the side.

TIME-SAVERS

■ **Do-ahead:** *The fruit can be cut up and the dressing made a short time ahead.*

Step 4

Values are approximate per serving: Calories: 150   Protein: 3 gm   Fat: 1 gm
Carbohydrates: 34 gm   Cholesterol: 2 mg   Sodium: 34 mg

Turkey Tabbouleh

Tabbouleh is a lemony, herbed grain salad from the Middle East.
Its main ingredient is bulgur, which is a specially processed form of cracked
wheat. The wheat kernels are steam-cooked and dried, and then cracked
into pieces. Because bulgur is pre-cooked, it can be prepared by steeping it (off the
heat) in boiling water for about 15 minutes; it can also be cooked like rice.

Working time: 25 minutes
Total time: 25 minutes

Turkey Tabbouleh

4 Servings

⅔ cup water	1 medium cucumber
⅔ cup bulgur	1 medium green bell pepper
3 cloves garlic, minced or crushed through a press	½ pound cooked turkey, unsliced
⅓ cup lemon juice	6 plum tomatoes or 9 whole canned tomatoes, well drained
½ teaspoon salt	2 tablespoons olive or other vegetable oil
⅓ cup (packed) parsley sprigs	
⅓ cup (packed) fresh dill sprigs or 1½ teaspoons dried	1 tablespoon grated lemon zest (optional; from about 2 lemons)
4 medium scallions	1 teaspoon pepper

Step 1

1 In a medium saucepan, bring the water, bulgur, garlic, 3 tablespoons of the lemon juice and the salt to a boil over medium-high heat. Cover and remove the pan from the heat. Let sit until the bulgur is tender and all the water has been absorbed, about 15 minutes.

2 Meanwhile, in a food processor, mince the parsley and dill; remove and set aside. In the same processor work bowl, coarsely chop the scallions. Add the cucumber and pulse on and off to coarsely chop; remove and set aside. Add the bell pepper and coarsely chop.

3 Cut the turkey into ¼-inch dice. Chop the tomatoes.

Step 3

4 In a large bowl, combine the bulgur, parsley, dill, scallions, cucumber, bell pepper, turkey and tomatoes. Add the remaining lemon juice, the olive oil, lemon zest (if using) and pepper. Toss to combine.

TIME-SAVERS

■ **Do-ahead:** *The individual components can be prepared or the whole salad assembled ahead of time.*

Step 4

Values are approximate per serving: Calories: 285 Protein: 22 gm Fat: 10 gm
Carbohydrates: 29 gm Cholesterol: 44 mg Sodium: 339 mg

Curried Pasta Salad with Cherry Tomatoes, Shrimp and Broccoli

▼

Efficiency is one of the keys to quick meals. Organize your ingredients before starting to cook, clean up as you go and, whenever possible, make one utensil, heat source or technique do double-duty. This recipe is a perfect example: As the pasta cooks, the vegetables are steamed in a colander placed over the boiling water; five minutes before the pasta is done, the shrimp are added and cooked right along with it.

Working time: 25 minutes
Total time: 25 minutes

6 Servings

½ pound medium shrimp
1 pint cherry tomatoes
1 large stalk broccoli
2 medium carrots
½ pound pasta twists
¼ cup packed cilantro sprigs
  (optional)
1 cup cottage cheese

1 cup plain yogurt
2 tablespoons lime juice
2 tablespoons curry powder
1 teaspoon grated lime zest
  (optional)
¼ teaspoon sugar
¼ teaspoon salt
⅛ teaspoon pepper

Step 2

1 Bring a large pot of water to a boil.

2 Meanwhile, shell and devein the shrimp. Halve the cherry tomatoes. Cut the broccoli and carrots into bite-size pieces.

3 Add the pasta to the boiling water and cook until al dente, 10 to 12 minutes, or according to package directions. While the pasta is cooking, place a colander over the boiling water and add the broccoli and carrots; cover the colander to steam the vegetables. Five minutes before the pasta is done, add the shrimp to the pasta cooking water and cook until opaque throughout.

4 Meanwhile, in a food processor, mince the cilantro (if using). Add the cottage cheese and process until smooth. Add the yogurt, lime juice, curry powder, lime zest (if using), sugar, salt and pepper, and process to blend.

Step 3

5 Drain the pasta and shrimp and place in a serving bowl. Add the cherry tomatoes, broccoli, carrots and curry sauce and toss lightly to combine. Serve the salad warm, at room temperature, or chilled.

TIME-SAVERS

■ **Do-ahead:** *All components of the salad can be prepared and cooked ahead, and the whole salad can be assembled ahead.*

Step 5

Values are approximate per serving: Calories: 265 Protein: 19 gm Fat: 4 gm
Carbohydrates: 39 gm Cholesterol: 55 mg Sodium: 327 mg

Apple Butternut Soup

▼

All the colors and flavors of autumn are embodied in this soup, which combines butternut squash, potatoes and applesauce. Since the potatoes are not peeled, be sure to choose the thin-skinned variety. If you don't have applesauce on hand, add four medium-size apples, peeled and cut into chunks, in Step 3. For a more delicately flavored soup, add ¼ cup milk or cream just before serving.

Working time: 15 minutes
Total time: 30 minutes

Apple Butternut Soup

4 Servings

1 small butternut squash (about 1 pound)
5 small white potatoes (about ½ pound total), unpeeled
1 medium onion

2 tablespoons butter
2½ cups chicken broth
¼ teaspoon salt
¼ teaspoon pepper
1½ cups unsweetened applesauce

1 Peel the squash and cut it into large cubes. Halve the potatoes. Cut the onion into thick slices.

2 In a medium saucepan, warm the butter over medium heat. Add the onion and cook until translucent, about 7 minutes.

3 Add the broth, squash, potatoes, salt and pepper. Increase the heat to medium-high and bring to a boil. Reduce the heat to medium-low, cover and simmer until the potatoes and squash are tender, about 15 minutes.

4 With a slotted spoon, remove the vegetables to a food processor and purée. Add the applesauce and pulse to combine. Return the purée to the broth in the saucepan and stir to combine. Serve hot.

TIME-SAVERS

■ **Do-ahead:** *The soup can be made ahead and reheated.*

Step 1

Step 1

Step 4

Values are approximate per serving: Calories: 199 Protein: 4 gm Fat: 7 gm
Carbohydrates: 33 gm Cholesterol: 16 mg Sodium: 820 mg

Gazpacho with Shrimp

To give this zesty soup the most appetizing—and authentic—texture,
leave the vegetables a bit chunky when you process them; they should not be puréed.
With the addition of shrimp—or strips of leftover cooked chicken, for an easy
variation—the soup becomes a meal. Traditionally a warm-weather favorite, gazpacho
is best served cold; a dollop of sour cream or yogurt makes a nice garnish.

Working time: 10 minutes
Total time: 10 minutes

Gazpacho with Shrimp

6 Servings

2 cloves garlic
8 sprigs cilantro or parsley
   (optional)
½ small cucumber, peeled
1 small green bell pepper
1 bunch scallions (6 to 8)
1 can (14½ ounces) whole
   tomatoes, with their juice
1 cup (¼ pound) frozen cooked
   baby shrimp, thawed

2 cans (11½ ounces each) low-
   sodium or regular vegetable juice
   cocktail
1 tablespoon red wine vinegar
½ teaspoon salt
¼ teaspoon black pepper
Pinch of ground cumin

Step 2

1 In a food processor or blender, mince the garlic and cilantro (if using).

2 Add the cucumber, green pepper and scallions and coarsely chop. Add the canned tomatoes with their juice and pulse briefly to coarsely chop.

Step 2

3 Turn the mixture into a large serving bowl and stir in the shrimp, vegetable juice, vinegar, salt, black pepper and cumin. Chill until ready to serve.

TIME-SAVERS

■ *Do-ahead: The whole dish can be made ahead of time and will be even better if it can be made far enough in advance to be thoroughly chilled.*

Step 3

Values are approximate per serving: Calories: 69   Protein: 6 gm   Fat: .43 gm
Carbohydrates: 11 gm   Cholesterol: 37 mg   Sodium: 367 mg

Lemony Spinach-Rice Soup

▼

*The combination of lemon juice and egg is a favorite in Greek cooking;
this recipe is based on Greek avgolemono—egg and lemon soup. The addition of
rice and spinach—also popular Greek ingredients—gives the soup a bit more
substance than the traditional recipe. The lemon flavor is quite intense (but pleasantly
so), especially if you use freshly squeezed lemon juice.*

Working time: 15 minutes
Total time: 30 minutes

Lemony Spinach-Rice Soup

6 Servings

6 cups chicken broth
1 cup water
⅔ cup raw rice
½ teaspoon pepper
½ pound fresh spinach or
  1 package (10 ounces) frozen
  chopped spinach, thawed

2 eggs
6 tablespoons lemon
  juice

1 In a medium saucepan, bring the broth and water to a boil over medium-high heat. Add the rice and pepper. Reduce the heat to medium-low, cover and simmer for 15 minutes.

2 Meanwhile, stem the spinach and tear the leaves into bite-size pieces. If using thawed frozen spinach, drain well and squeeze out any excess moisture.

3 In a small bowl, lightly beat the eggs. After the rice has cooked for 15 minutes, remove about ¼ cup of the hot broth and whisk it into the beaten egg. Beat the warmed egg mixture into the hot soup.

4 Add the spinach and the lemon juice and cook the soup over medium-low heat, stirring constantly, for 5 minutes; do not allow the soup to simmer or the egg will curdle.

5 Serve the soup hot.

Step 3

Step 3

Step 4

Values are approximate per serving: Calories: 137 Protein: 7 gm Fat: 3 gm
Carbohydrates: 20 gm Cholesterol: 71 mg Sodium: 1033 mg

Tomato-Clam Chowder with Garlic Crostini

▼

*Fans of tomato-based Manhattan clam chowder will love this version,
in which garlicky crostini (large croutons) take the place of the usual oyster
crackers. The crostini are baked while the chowder is on the stove, and
are served alongside bowls of the chowder. Or, if desired, place the crostini in
shallow soup bowls and ladle the chowder over them.*

Working time: 20 minutes
Total time: 30 minutes

Tomato-Clam Chowder
with Garlic Crostini

4 Servings

1 can (16 ounces) whole tomatoes,
  with their juice
1 cup chicken broth
2 cloves garlic, minced or crushed
  through a press
½ teaspoon sugar
¼ teaspoon pepper
2 medium all-purpose potatoes

4 scallions
½ cup bottled clam juice or
  chicken broth
2 teaspoons cornstarch
2 tablespoons olive oil
8 slices (½-inch-thick) French or
  Italian bread
1 can (6½ ounces) clams, drained

Step 2

1 In a medium saucepan, combine the tomatoes and their juice, the chicken broth, half the garlic, the sugar and pepper. Break the tomatoes up with a spoon. Bring the mixture to a boil, covered, over medium-high heat.

2 Meanwhile, peel and cube the potatoes. Add the potatoes to the boiling tomato-broth mixture. Reduce the heat to medium-low, cover and simmer until the potatoes are tender, about 15 minutes.

3 Meanwhile, coarsely chop the scallions. In a small bowl, blend the clam juice with the cornstarch.

4 Preheat the oven to 400°. Line a baking sheet with foil.

5 In a small skillet, warm the oil over medium heat. Add the remaining garlic and cook, stirring, until the garlic is fragrant, 1 to 2 minutes. Remove the pan from the heat.

Step 6

6 Brush both sides of the bread with the garlic oil and place them on the foil-lined baking sheet. Bake for 8 minutes, or until golden.

7 Bring the soup back to a boil over medium-high heat. Stir the clam juice-cornstarch mixture to reblend and add it to the boiling broth. Cook, stirring, until the liquid has thickened slightly, 1 to 2 minutes.

8 Add the scallions and clams. Serve hot with the crostini on the side.

TIME-SAVERS

■ *Microwave tip: In a microwave-safe casserole, combine all of the chowder ingredients except the scallions, clam juice, cornstarch and clams. Cover and cook at 100%, stirring twice, for 15 minutes, or until the potatoes are tender. Blend the cornstarch and clam juice and add it to the casserole along with the clams and scallions. Cook, uncovered, at 100%, stirring once, for 4 minutes, or until the liquid has thickened. (Prepare the crostini as instructed above.)*

Values are approximate per serving: Calories: 290 Protein: 13 gm Fat: 9 gm
Carbohydrates: 40 gm Cholesterol: 17 mg Sodium: 731 mg

Step 8

Tangy Curried Zucchini Soup

Although zucchini has many virtues (it is widely available and usually inexpensive), it takes a bit of imagination to wake up the vegetable's subtle flavor. This puréed soup is sparked with garlic, basil and curry powder, and enriched with sour cream and yogurt. These ingredients add up to a lot of flavor, but not a lot of calories. The same technique could be used with other vegetables, such as cooked winter squash or sweet potatoes.

Working time: 20 minutes
Total time: 30 minutes

306

Tangy Curried Zucchini Soup

4 Servings

3 cups low-sodium or regular
  chicken broth
3 cloves garlic, minced or crushed
  through a press
3 tablespoons curry powder
¼ teaspoon pepper
2 large zucchini (about 1 pound)

4 scallions
3 tablespoons chopped fresh basil
  or 1½ teaspoons dried
6 tablespoons plain yogurt
2 tablespoons sour cream
2 tablespoons cornstarch

1 In a medium saucepan, bring the chicken broth, garlic, curry powder and pepper to a boil over medium-high heat.

2 Meanwhile, cut the zucchini into 1-inch lengths. Coarsely chop the scallions. Chop the basil.

Step 2

3 Add the zucchini, scallions and basil to the boiling broth. Reduce the heat to low, cover and simmer until the zucchini is tender, about 10 minutes.

4 With a slotted spoon, remove the solids to a food processor and process to a purée.

5 In a large bowl, blend together 4 tablespoons of the yogurt, the sour cream and cornstarch. Add the puréed vegetables and stir to combine.

6 Return the zucchini mixture to the saucepan. Bring the soup to a boil over medium heat and cook, stirring, until slightly thickened, 1 to 2 minutes.

7 Ladle the soup into bowls and garnish with the remaining yogurt (1½ teaspoons per serving).

Step 4

TIME-SAVERS

■ ***Microwave tip:*** *In a 2-quart microwave-safe casserole, combine all of the ingredients except the yogurt, sour cream and cornstarch; reduce the chicken broth to only 2½ cups. Cover and cook at 100% until the zucchini is tender, about 12 minutes. Proceed with Steps 4 and 5 as described above. Return the soup to the casserole, cover and cook at 100% until the mixture is heated through but not boiling, about 3 minutes.*

■ ***Do-ahead:*** *The soup can be made ahead through Step 4. The soup can also be made completely ahead and served chilled.*

Values are approximate per serving: Calories: 107   Protein: 5 gm   Fat: 4 gm
Carbohydrates: 15 gm   Cholesterol: 4 mg   Sodium: 66 mg

Step 6

Modern Minestrone

The full flavor of this soup is unquestionably old-fashioned. It's the pared-down preparation time that makes the minestrone modern: canned beans and frozen peas cut the cooking time to about 20 minutes. If you're using frozen peas from a 10-ounce box, store the remaining peas in a plastic bag. Or add them to a green salad and serve it with the soup.

Working time: 5 minutes
Total time: 25 minutes

Modern Minestrone

6 Servings

3½ cups beef broth	1 medium onion
1½ cups water	1 large carrot
1 can (16 ounces) crushed tomatoes	3 cloves garlic
1 teaspoon basil	1 cup frozen peas
¼ teaspoon pepper	1 cup elbow macaroni
1 can (15 ounces) black beans	⅓ cup grated Parmesan cheese

1 In a 4-quart covered saucepan, bring the broth, water, tomatoes, basil and pepper to a boil over high heat.

2 Meanwhile, drain the beans in a colander, rinse under cold running water and drain well.

Step 2

3 In a food processor, coarsely chop the onion, carrot and garlic.

4 Add the onion, carrot, garlic, drained beans, peas and macaroni to the boiling broth mixture. Reduce the heat to medium-low, cover and simmer, stirring occasionally, until the macaroni is al dente, about 12 minutes.

5 Serve with grated Parmesan cheese on the side.

Step 3

TIME-SAVERS

■ *Do-ahead: The minestrone can be made ahead of time.*

Step 4

Values are approximate per serving: Calories: 226 Protein: 13 gm Fat: 3 gm
Carbohydrates: 37 gm Cholesterol: 4 mg Sodium: 922 mg

Fast Fish Chowder

The fish used in this quick chowder is scrod, a mild-flavored, firm-fleshed white fish. If scrod is not available, you can substitute any similar fish such as cod, halibut or haddock. You can also use frozen fish fillets (thawed) instead of fresh fish. To trim the calorie count of this recipe even further, use 1% or 2% milk in place of some or all of the whole milk. Serve the chowder with unsalted saltines.

Working time: 15 minutes
Total time: 25 minutes

Fast Fish Chowder

4 Servings

2 medium all-purpose potatoes (about 1 pound)	½ pound scrod fillet, or other firm-fleshed white fish, such as cod, halibut or haddock
2 medium carrots	
2 stalks celery	½ teaspoon salt
1 medium onion	¼ teaspoon pepper
1 can (13¾ ounces) chicken broth	1 cup milk
1 cup water	

1 Peel the potatoes and cut them into ½-inch dice. Cut the carrots and celery into ½-inch dice. Coarsely chop the onion.

2 In a large saucepan, bring the broth and water to a boil over medium-high heat.

3 Add the potatoes and onion, reduce the heat to medium-low, cover and simmer until the potatoes are tender, about 15 minutes, stirring occasionally.

4 Meanwhile, cut the fish into ¾-inch cubes, removing any bones.

5 Increase the heat to medium-high and bring the liquid to a boil. Add the scrod, carrots, celery, salt and pepper.

6 Reduce the heat to medium-low, cover the pan and simmer until the fish flakes easily, 5 to 10 minutes.

7 Stir in the milk and cook until heated through, 1 to 2 minutes. Serve hot.

TIME-SAVERS

■ *Do-ahead: The potatoes, carrots, celery, onion and fish can be cut up ahead. The chowder can be made ahead through Step 3, cooking the potatoes until they are not quite tender. Then, bring the chowder back to a boil before proceeding with the recipe.*

Values are approximate per serving: Calories: 192 Protein: 15 gm Fat: 4 gm
Carbohydrates: 24 gm Cholesterol: 33 mg Sodium: 937 mg

Step 1

Step 4

Step 7

South-of-the-Border Black Bean Soup

▼

Black bean soup is one of the most comforting soups ever created. This version, seasoned with chili, oregano, garlic and cilantro, has a Mexican flavor. A dollop of sour cream makes it even richer and smoother, but you can leave it out, or substitute plain yogurt. Canned beans should always be rinsed and drained before they are used; this substantially reduces the sodium content of the soup.

Working time: 10 minutes
Total time: 30 minutes

South-of-the-Border Black Bean Soup

6 Servings

2 cans (16 ounces each) black beans
1 package (10 ounces) frozen corn
1 medium onion
1 tablespoon vegetable oil
2 cloves garlic, minced or crushed through a press

2¾ cups chicken broth
1 tablespoon chili powder
1½ teaspoons oregano
Pinch of cayenne
1 bay leaf
¼ cup chopped cilantro (optional)
½ cup sour cream (optional)

Step 2

1 Place the black beans and the corn in a colander. Hold under cold running water to rinse the beans and thaw the corn; drain well. Coarsely chop the onion.

2 In a large saucepan, warm the oil over medium-high heat until hot but not smoking. Add the onion and garlic and cook until the onion begins to brown, about 5 minutes.

3 Add the drained beans and corn, the chicken broth, chili powder, oregano, cayenne and bay leaf. Cover and bring the mixture to a boil. Reduce the heat to medium-low, cover and simmer for 15 minutes. Remove the bay leaf.

Step 3

4 Just before serving, remove about 1½ cups of the solids and purée them in a blender or food processor. Return the purée to the soup.

5 Serve the soup with a sprinkling of cilantro and a dollop of sour cream, if desired.

TIME-SAVERS

■ *Microwave tip: In a 3-quart microwave-safe casserole, combine the onion, oil and garlic; cover and cook at 100% for 3 minutes. Stir in the rinsed beans, corn, chicken broth, chili powder, oregano, cayenne and bay leaf. Re-cover and cook at 100% for 8 minutes, or until the mixture comes to a boil. Cook at 50% for 10 minutes, stirring occasionally, to blend the flavors. Purée the soup as described above.*

■ *Do-ahead: The whole soup can be made ahead and reheated.*

Values are approximate per serving: Calories: 237 Protein: 13 gm Fat: 4 gm Carbohydrates: 40 gm Cholesterol: 0 mg Sodium: 835 mg

Step 4

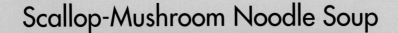

Scallop-Mushroom Noodle Soup

▼

This Asian take on a hearty noodle soup combines vegetables, scallops, and Chinese noodles in a light but flavorful broth. The noodles used here are made of wheat flour and water and are sold fresh or dried in Asian markets and in some supermarkets. If you can't find them, substitute spaghettini, angel hair or other very thin noodles, allowing extra cooking time according to the package directions.

Working time: 15 minutes
Total time: 25 minutes

4 Servings

**3 quarter-size slices (¼ inch thick)
  fresh ginger, unpeeled**
¼ pound mushrooms
3 scallions
**½ pound bay scallops or sea
  scallops**
4 cups low-sodium chicken broth

1 teaspoon Oriental sesame oil
¼ teaspoon red pepper flakes
½ pound Chinese noodles
**¼ pound bean sprouts (soy bean
  or mung bean)**
¼ pound snow peas

1 Bring a large pot of water to a boil.

2 Meanwhile, shred or mince the ginger. Cut the mushrooms into thin slices. Cut the scallions into slivers 1½ inches long. If using sea scallops, cut them into quarters.

Step 2

3 In a large saucepan, bring the chicken broth, ginger, sesame oil and red pepper flakes to a boil over medium-high heat.

4 Add the noodles to the boiling water and cook until al dente, about 3 minutes, or according to package directions.

5 When the broth comes to a boil, add the scallops, bean sprouts, snow peas and mushrooms. Reduce the heat to low, cover and cook until the vegetables are just tender, 1 to 2 minutes. Add the scallions and cook an additional 30 seconds.

6 Drain the noodles and divide them among individual soup bowls. Dividing evenly, ladle the broth and scallop-vegetable mixture over the noodles.

Step 5

TIME-SAVERS

■ ***Do-ahead:*** *The vegetables can be cut up and the seasoned broth (Step 3) made ahead. Bring the broth back to a boil before proceeding with Steps 5 and 6.*

Values are approximate per serving: Calories: 332   Protein: 22 gm   Fat: 4 gm
Carbohydrates: 51 gm   Cholesterol: 19 mg   Sodium: 153 mg

Step 6

INDEX